Walks & Rambles in the

UPPER CONNECTICUT RIVER VALLEY

The almost twin Percy Peaks dominate the landscape above the upper Amonoosuc River.

Walks & Rambles in the

UPPER CONNECTICUT RIVER VALLEY

From Quebec to the Massachusetts Border

MARY L. KIBLING

Photographs by the author

A Walks & Rambles™ Guide

Backcountry Publications
The Countryman Press, Inc.
Woodstock, Vermont

*To Elizabeth Parker, a faithful and joyful com-
panion and friend, with deepest gratitude.*

An Invitation to the Reader

Over time trails can be rerouted and signs and landmarks altered. If you find that
changes have occurred along the walks described in this book, please let us know
so that corrections may be made in future editions. The author and publisher also
welcome other comments and suggestions. Address all correspondence to:

Editor
Walks and Rambles™ Series
Backcountry Publications
P.O. Box 175
Woodstock, VT 05091

Library of Congress Cataloging-in-Publication Data

Kibling, Mary L.
    Walks & rambles in the upper Connecticut River Valley : from Quebec to
    the Massachusetts border / Mary L. Kibling ; photographs by the
    author.
        p.   cm.—(A Walks & rambles guide)
    Bibliography: p.
    ISBN 0-88150-140-9 : $9.95
        1.   Hiking—Connecticut River Valley—Guide-books.   2. Connecticut
    River Valley—Description and travel—Guide-books.   I. Title.
    II. Series.
    GV199.42.C83K53   1989   89-34607
    917.4—dc20   CIP

Published by Backcountry Publications
A division of The Countryman Press, Inc.
Woodstock, Vermont 05091

Printed in the United States of America
Typesetting by NK Graphics
Design by Ann Aspell
Layout by Anne Davis
Maps and calligraphy by Alex Wallach
Photographs on pages 65, 120, 125, and 129 by Nancy-Jane Jackson

Acknowledgments

One of the more exciting things about writing this book has been the enthusiasm and encouragement of so many people who made the work interesting, educational, and fun. Sincere thanks go to: The Green Mountain Club's Brian Fitzgerald, who helped me get started; Jeff Wallner and the ladies at The Society for the Protection of New Hampshire Forests; the Capital Area Chapter of the Audubon Society of New Hampshire; the Dartmouth Bookstore People; the Dartmouth Outing Club, and a nice lady at the Montshire Museum in Hanover; the Chapmans at Chapman's Store in Fairlee, Vermont; the folks at the Hulbert Outdoor Center on Lake Morey; Paul Levesque, the ranger at Maidstone State Park, and Susan Fisher at the Vermont Department of Forest, Parks, and Recreation; Mr. Guy Bemis, who spent a whole day kindling my interest in the history of the Connecticut River Valley and especially Walpole, New Hampshire; Richard Peloquin at the Horatio Colony Trust in Keene; Stephen Dehl at the United States Customs Station in Pittsburgh, New Hampshire; Marjorie and Daniel Doan, Donald Snyder, Virginia Parker, Lucia Kittredge, the Garden Club of Fitzwilliam, Everett Towne and the Vermont Land Trust, numerous town and state librarians, a supportive publisher and staff, and a most helpful editor.

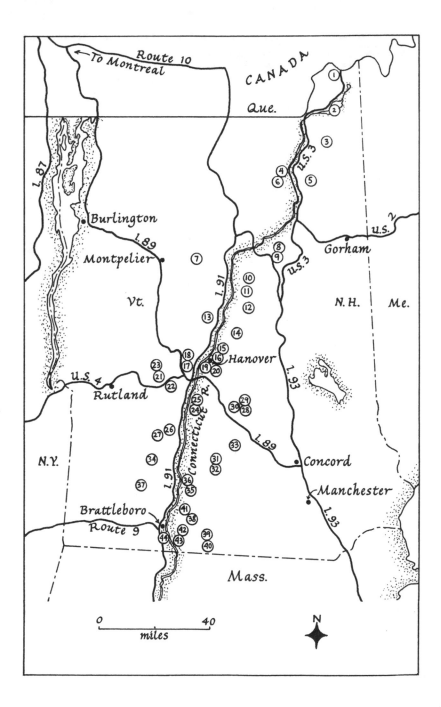

Table of Contents

Introduction   1

NEW HAMPSHIRE'S NORTH COUNTRY AND VERMONT'S NORTHEAST KINGDOM   7

1. Fourth Connecticut Lake   8

2. Mount Magalloway   12
3. Table Rock   16
4. Brunswick Springs   20
5. Percy Peaks   23
6. Maidstone State Park   27
7. Kettle Pond   31
8. Bretzfelder Memorial Park—Four Seasons Trail   35
9. Red Barns Trail   39
10. Autumn Wildflowers at Scotland Brook   42

THE APPALACHIAN TRAIL AND NEARBY GENTLE HILLS   47

11. Black Mountain   48
12. Blueberry Mountain   51
13. The Palisades   54
14. Mount Cube   58
15. Holt's Ledge   62
16. Moose Mountain   66
17. Gile Mountain   70
18. Happy Hill   72
19. Pine Park   77
20. Velvet Rocks   80
21. Mount Tom   83
22. Mount Peg   86
23. Carl's Walk   89

SUNAPEE, DARTMOUTH, AND THE SHADOWS OF MOUNT ASCUTNEY

SUNAPEE, DARTMOUTH, AND THE SHADOWS
OF MOUNT ASCUTNEY   93

24. Saint-Gaudens National Historic Site   94
25. Blow-Me-Down Natural Area   98
26. The Pinnacle   102
27. Springweather Nature Area   104
28. The Bunker Place   109
29. The Cascades   114
30. The Philbrick-Cricenti Bog   118
31. Lucia's Lookout   122
32. Bear Pond Beaver Dam   127
33. The Newbury Cut   130
34. The Cheese Factory Trail   134

BELLOWS FALLS SOUTH TO
MASSACHUSETTS   137

35. High Blue   138
36. A Walk Around Historic Walpole   141
37. Ledges Overlook   146
38. Horatio Colony Land Trust   149
39. Little Monadnock Mountain   155
40. Rhododendron State Park   158
41. Chesterfield Gorge   161
42. The Kilburn Loop Trail in Pisgah State Park   164
43. Wantastiquet Mountain   169
44. The Sunrise Trail–Fort Dummer State Park   172

Introduction

THE CONNECTICUT RIVER BEGINS ITS 407-MILE JOURNEY from a tiny pond on the United States–Canada border at Pittsburgh, New Hampshire. It flows through dammed lakes and rapids that once carried lumber south to great mills. Sometimes it is quiet, sometimes white, sometimes narrow, sometimes wide. It meanders and bends around ox-bow curves through fertile farm country. It rushes over falls, past industrial cities that depend upon the water's force for electrical power. It travels through the states of New Hampshire, Vermont, Massachusetts, and Connecticut to empty, finally, into the Long Island Sound, just south of Old Saybrook, Connecticut.

American Indians who lived along the river's shores named the river Quinnitukut, or "Long River." Adriaen Block, a Dutch navigator, was the first white man to discover the river. He explored it in 1614, and named it De Verche Riviere, or "Freshwater River." It bore this name until the territory was claimed by English settlers, who called it by the Indian name, which was spelled many different ways before it was eventually given today's spelling.

The Upper Valley is commonly thought of as the middle sections of New Hampshire and Vermont. In this book we have stretched it northward along the river to the Canadian border, in order to include its source, and southward to the Massachusetts border, in order to include walks and history we couldn't pass by.

To walk along the river's banks, down the valley's old roads and trails, or up its sheltering mountains, is to ramble through scenes of much of our land's early history. There is evidence that the Connecticut River Valley was inhabited as long as eight thousand years ago. After 1000 A.D. Indians began to live in villages, or sachems, throughout northern New England, and by 1600 most of what we know as Vermont and New Hampshire was inhabited by the Western Abenaki. The Sokoki occupied the Upper Valley. Until the white settlers came, no written record was kept of the lives of the Indians, so our knowledge of times before then is limited.

Most of the white pioneers of this region came from Connecticut. Discouraged from farming by Connecticut's rocky soil, and allured by the profits to be made in fur trade with the Indians, they pushed northward. The area was heavily wooded at that time. Towns and

1

The upper Connecticut River meanders through fertile farm country.

self-sufficient farms were built on hills, because the dense forest land along the river banks was too wet to farm. Later, when the land had been cleared and the soil was subsequently drier, the settlers moved down to the fertile shores of the river, often bringing their buildings with them. Newfane, Vermont is an example of a town that was built on the heights and then brought down, building by building, to where it now stands.

Grants of land for the settlement of a town usually stipulated that a number of acres of the great pine trees be reserved for ships' masts for the Royal Navy. The mighty pines were floated down the river to the sea, to be shipped to England. Major settlement of the valley towns took place in the mid-1700s, after the end of the French and Indian Wars. The region soon became prosperous, as can be surmised by the elegant homes still in use, built by early successful farmers, merchants, and lawyers in towns such as Orford, New Hampshire, Norwich, Vermont, and Walpole, New Hampshire.

The valley's new inhabitants made significant contributions to industry, including the development of mass production—first for guns, then for farm implements, and later for the woolen mills, which thrived until cotton from the southern states and cheap imports from abroad killed the market for New England woolens.

Experimental ventures in the valley's educational institutions became important to the development of the nation's educational system. Eleazar Wheelock founded Dartmouth College and trained white missionaries to educate Indians. Though the college charter was given for the purpose of educating Indians, not many students took advantage of that opportunity. Nathan Smith founded the medical school at Dartmouth College, and contributed to the founding of medical schools at Yale University, Bowdoin College, and the University of Vermont. The Noyes Academy in Canaan, New Hampshire was among the first schools in the country to encourage the education of blacks beyond grammar school levels. The Tilden Female Seminary in West Lebanon, New Hampshire was one of America's first girls' schools to have its own building. Justin Smith Morrill of Strafford, Vermont presented the Land Grant Act to Congress in 1862. Its passage paved the way for the Land Grant Colleges, whose purpose was to educate people in agriculture and "the mechanical arts."

Logging in the far north began in earnest in the 1800s, with the Connecticut Valley Lumber Company dominating operations in northeastern Vermont and the Connecticut Lakes area in New Hampshire. The Connecticut River log drives were among the largest in the country, transporting their precious cargo from the northern lakes to mills at Holyoke and Mount Tom in Massachusetts. Log jams damaged bridges, created floods, and cluttered farm fields. The last drive of long logs took place in 1915. Smaller pulpwood log drives continued until 1940. Today's travelers in the north country meet heavily loaded trucks carrying logs to their destinations.

The French and Indian Wars saw bands of Indian raiders move their captives up the valley to Canada. The first casualty of the American Revolution was recorded in Westminster, Vermont, one month before the "shot heard 'round the world" at Concord, Massachusetts. During the Civil War there were stations of the Underground Railroad for escaped slaves traveling north. Mica from local mines went into the construction of bombsights for World War II aircraft.

Fine arts flourished in the Upper Valley in the nineteenth century. Augustus Saint-Gaudens, one of America's most important sculptors,

3

lived and worked in Cornish, New Hampshire; his home and studios are now a National Historic Shrine. The painter Maxfield Parrish lived in Plainfield, New Hampshire. Rudyard Kipling wrote his Jungle Books while living in Brattleboro, Vermont.

Tourism first blossomed in New Hampshire and Vermont because the many mineral springs in the Connecticut River Valley were thought to have curative powers. Hotels and vacation colonies sprang up where the people who first sought the cures had stayed in boarding houses. Today the Upper Valley offers tourists its scenic beauty, charming inns and hotels, and opportunities for the adventurous to canoe on the river, camp, bicycle, ride horseback, fish, hunt, and ski. And of course there are walks and hikes of all levels of difficulty and ease.

We have traveled the valley on both sides of the river, from Canada to the Massachusetts border, and have found a great many places to walk. We give you here only a sample of what we found. When you become addicted to the valley, as we have, stop in at the local village store, gas station, historical society, or nature center, to find information about other walks in each area you visit. We also suggest that you read *The Day Hiker's Guide to Vermont* (Green Mountain Club), *White Mountain Guide* (Appalachian Mountain Club), *50 Hikes in Vermont, 50 Hikes in the White Mountains,* and *50 More Hikes in New Hampshire* (all three—Backcountry Publications). These books will expand your walking horizons.

WHAT TO TAKE WITH YOU

A daypack frees your arms, and is almost a must for even the shortest walk. You should always carry water to drink, a rain or wind jacket, a sweater, a lunch or snack, and some emergency equipment such as moleskin for a blister, a bandana for a quick sling, and an elastic bandage for a turned ankle. Sturdy walking shoes or boots, preferably water-repellent, will allow you a more comfortable walk. I carry in my pack a small bag containing a knife, compass, whistle, matches, candle, flashlight, and mirror. A brimmed hat protects you from sun, bugs, and rain. A knitted hat and mittens are valuable in cooler weather. You might enjoy a camera, binoculars, and field guides for nature study. Most of these walks are fun in the winter on skis or snowshoes, so don't limit yourself to warmer weather. In the late spring and summer you'll be happy that you brought along insect repellent. Last, but not least, take a companion. You really shouldn't walk alone. If you must walk alone, please let somebody know that you're going and when you expect to return—then be sure to let that person know when you're back.

MAPS, TRAILS, WALKING TIMES AND DISTANCES

The walks in this book are organized into four sections, including both sides of the Connecticut River. The maps are simple sketches; for greater detail, USGS Survey Maps of each area can be helpful. The trails are usually indicated in the field by blazes (oblongs of paint on trees or rocks), metal rectangles about three inches square nailed to trees, or by rock cairns (small to large piles of rocks) to the side or in the middle of trails.

These walks and rambles are planned for families with small children, people not interested in scaling great heights, and people just out for a peaceful stroll. Most of them are not difficult. There are a couple of "real" hikes, and they are specified as such. Distance and walking times are round-trip, and are approximate so that you can plan your trip to include lunch by a stream or on top of a hill, and so that you can enjoy the trees and flowers, listen to the birds, study old cellar holes, and reflect upon the past. You may also become more conscious of what's happening to our environment, and consider our future.

BIBLIOGRAPHY

Appalachian Mountain Club. *White Mountain Guide* (Boston: Appalachian Mountain Club, 1983)

Bachman, Ben. *Upstream* (Boston: Houghton Mifflin, 1985)

Doan, Daniel. *Fifty Hikes in the White Mountains,* 3rd ed., updated (Woodstock, Vermont: Backcountry Publications, 1988)

Doan, Daniel. *Fifty More Hikes in New Hampshire,* rev. ed., updated (Woodstock, Vermont: Backcountry Publications, 1988)

The Green Mountain Club. *Day Hiker's Guide to Vermont* (Montpelier, Vermont: The Green Mountain Club, 1987)

Hard, Walter. *The Connecticut* (New York: Rinehart & Co., 1947)

Jager, Ronald and Grace. *Historical Pillsbury* (Concord: NH, The Society for the Protection of New Hampshire Forests, 1976)

Pike, Robert E. *Tall Trees, Tough Men* (New York: W.W. Norton & Co., 1967)

Pinette, Richard E. *Northwoods Echoes* (Colebrook, NH: Liebl Printing, 1986)

Sadlier, Hugh and Heather. *Fifty Hikes in Vermont*, 3rd. ed., updated (Woodstock, Vermont: Backcountry Publications, 1988)

Schweiker, Roioli. *25 Ski Tours in New Hampshire* (Woodstock, Vermont: Backcountry Publications, 1988)

Wikoff, Jerold. *The Upper Valley* (Chelsea, Vermont: Chelsea Green, 1985)

Numerous booklets and pamphlets distributed by the Parks and Recreation Departments of New Hampshire and Vermont

Town histories

MAP SYMBOLS

Ⓟ	parking area
—	road
●●●	main trail
·····	side trail or alternate route
⌒	bridge
⌂	shelter
🪑	bench
▰▰▰	stone wall
♉	orchard
☼	view
🗼	tower (observation, fire, etc.)
▲	point of elevation
⏥	boulder
■	building
†	cemetery
⚐	Appalachian Trail
X	point of interest
===	abandoned road or dirt road

New Hampshire's North Country and Vermont's Northeast Kingdom

1. Fourth Connecticut Lake

Walking distance: 2 miles
Walking time: 2 hours
Pittsburg, New Hampshire

YOU REALLY SHOULD BEGIN AT THE BEGINNING OF things, don't you agree? The Fourth Lake, in our magnificent North Country, is the source of the Connecticut River. It hides, deep in the forest, behind the U.S. Customs House, with the U.S.–Canada border leading you to it. It's a shallow pond, sheltered by dark balsams and bright green–leaved hardwoods. Dainty buckbean flowers grow at its edge. There's a beaver dam at its outlet. From this backwoods tarn, the longest river in New England begins its journey to the sea. The drive up the river, past the first three Connecticut Lakes, takes you through spectacular scenery. This is splendid vacation country if you like peace and quiet. The friendly people at the information office in Pittsburg can help you find lodgings or campgrounds to please most tastes.

ACCESS

Proceed on US 3 to the Customs House just south of the border from Chartiereville, Quebec, and park your car there. Sign in with the customs officer, who will point you to a rather indistinct trail to your right, in back of the customs building. It has been rumored that there will soon be trail signs and a clearer path to the lake, but these improvements have not been made as of this writing.

The walk is fairly rugged. You should have long pants, a long-sleeved shirt, a hat, rain gear, and a snack and drink. If you go in winter, please take a map and compass and, of course, warm clothes. You'll need boots or sturdy shoes in any season.

TRAIL

You can get in to Fourth Lake in less time than we've given you, but there are so many things to see both on the way and when you get

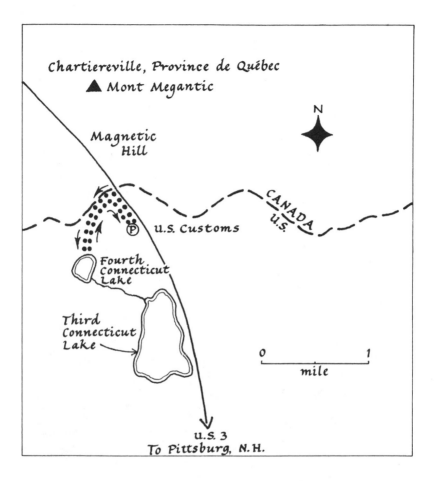

Chartiereville, Province de Québec
▲ Mont Megantic

N

Magnetic
Hill

CANADA
U.S.

Ⓟ U.S. Customs

Fourth
Connecticut
Lake

Third
Connecticut
Lake

0 ————————— 1
mile

U.S. 3
To Pittsburg, N.H.

there that you should take time to enjoy them. Turn left, from the Customs House, and walk north-northwest to a set of steep slate steps. In about five minutes you'll see that you're on the path that marks the border between the U.S. and Canada. There's a government marker in the rock at the top of the hill. The trail levels out to wind through beds of skunk currant, clintonia, and wood sorrel, which blossoms in June. Painted trillium lift their little white heads to the sun. You might see deep moose tracks in the mud. There are beds of bunchberry and Carolina spring beauty. The balsam forest smells delicious.

In about ten minutes you'll approach a steep rise, and if you look

9

You might see Moose tracks in the mud.

back you'll see the tiny town of Chartiereville in Quebec, with Mont Megantic in the background. The low branch of a wild cherry tree gives you a handhold for pulling yourself up a long rock. Keep along the path through heartleaf birch trees, past another border marker, and bear left around a giant anthill that's about five feet in diameter. Thousands of ants scurry over it, busy with their work.

Walk fifteen minutes more and go right over a fallen tree trunk, then left west-northwest to push aside the branches of two spruces that nearly block your path. The trail curves left, then right again. Go left at a yellow witness post sign on a tree to your left, then slightly downhill into an old forest. Whenever you have to cross downed trees, search diligently beyond the trees to find the path again.

You should now be able to see the lake through the trees and to follow the path to its shore. Notice the buckbane blossoms in the shallow water during June. Visit the beaver dam at the far end of the pond if the shore is not too wet between here and there. Sit a while and reflect on the mighty river, its humble beginnings up in the woods, the log drives down below, fishermen wading or paddling its peaceful reaches, the farms it irrigates, cows in riverside pastures, electric power provided by faster waters farther south, factories drawing their mouth. This river has flowed through fields, towns and cities, dams and lakes, and the history of our country from glaciers, to Indians, to white settlers, to us.

Return the way you came. Be careful not to lose the trail in places where bushes and trees have grown up or fallen across your path.

If you're staying nearby, go into Canada and drive on to Magnetic Hill, where you'll feel your car pulled backwards uphill. Visit the Mont Megantic Observatoire. Visitors are encouraged from July 1 through Labor Day. Quebec Universities students study the skies through the telescope here, and you can, too, if you make reservations for a Saturday night. Ask about this opportunity at either customs house.

2. Mount Magalloway

Walking distance: 4½ miles
Walking time: 3½ hours
Pittsburg, New Hampshire

THIS MOUNTAIN LOOMS OVER A BRANCH OF THE
dead Diamond River, about 8 miles east of the First Connecticut Lake
off US 3, in a wilderness cut only by logging roads. You won't see a
lot of people, though you might see a moose or catch a glimpse of the
soft white tail of a deer as she bounds into the woods near you. You
might pass a log-laden truck, and you will pass a lone cabin labeled
Ralphie's Paradise.

ACCESS

Drive 4.7 miles on US 3 past the First Connecticut Lake Dam, turn
southeast off the highway, and in 1 mile cross the Connecticut River
on a wooden bridge. Signs on the right, toward the lake, tell you that
you might catch salmon here, but the minimum size you can keep is
fifteen inches. On the north side of the bridge there's a sign that says
"No Fishing." Take a right at the fork at the end of the bridge. Travel
.9 mile to a second fork, then go left .7 mile to a third fork. You'll
see signs to the Lookout Station and Magalloway Lookout Tower.
Cross the height of land on the gravel road. At 2.4 miles from the
third fork, look for more signs and a right-hand turn. Make the turn
and drive approximately 1.8 miles to a clearcut area, where there is
space to park and a sign telling you that no vehicles are allowed beyond
this point.

Park here to begin your hike. Two brown-and-yellow signs with
arrows point at the mountain—*do not follow these signs*. Instead, walk
the road straight beyond another sign at the side of the road that
continues in the direction in which you came.

TRAIL

Walk southwest past the sign, straight ahead on the road, which soon

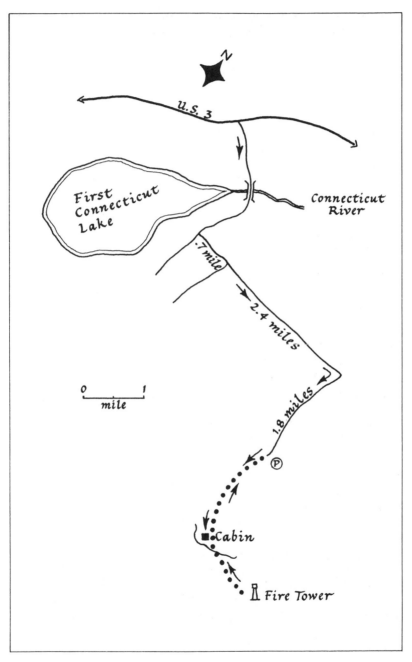

N

U.S. 3

First
Connecticut
Lake

Connecticut
River

.7 mile

2.4 miles

0   1
   mile

1.8 miles

Ⓟ

■Cabin

⛫ Fire Tower

13

bends south toward the mountain on your left. If you look sharply up to the summit you can see the fire tower you're headed for.

Moose and deer tracks in the mud lead you along the way. Bunchberry grows on the banks, and meadow rue waves its long stems by the side of the road. Great hollow-stalked cow parsnip blooms above its large, flat, notched leaves. Tall spruces accent the birches and maples on both sides of you.

After about half an hour the road goes gradually uphill. It's lined with flowers: horsetail, foam flower, Indian poke. Yellow-blossomed rough cinquefoil grows in the middle of the road. There's a sign to the tower nailed high up on a tree to your right. Opposite and to the left, orange ribbons tied around trees indicate that some trail arrives here from somewhere in that forest. Blue violets grow in a clump. The road curves to the right, and in fifteen minutes more you come upon a cabin. Just past it there's a pipe from a spring spilling water into a small stream. It invites you to stop a spell and enjoy a cool mountain drink.

The road ends a few steps farther on. The trail goes to the right and is nearly perpendicular for .7 mile. The flora look as though you've gone back in time two weeks as you see flowers in bloom that have gone by down below. Clintonia, Canada mayflower, and wood sorrel treat you to a second springtime.

Take it easy up the steep climb, and rejoice in the fact that this is the short part of your walk. It doesn't last long. Look back to catch your breath and you'll take in a fine view of First Connecticut Lake and the hills beyond it, far beneath you. Did you know that these lakes are really dammed portions of the river? They were dammed so that logs could be floated down the river, and are important to the economy of the North Country.

Ahead of you, at the top of the hill, there's sunlight on the grass as the forest opens up. It's all green grass and bunchberry right to the sky. Then the old road winds around to the fire warden's camp and a wide open space with a massive fire tower above you. Wildflowers in little gardens decorate the bases of the trees in the small park. Wonderful views entertain you for lunch and reward you for that last breath-stealing effort.

Return the way you came. It's a relaxing walk down to your car. Maybe a moose will appear at the side of US 3 as you travel south.

14

Stop a spell and enjoy a cool mountain drink.

3. Table Rock

Walking distance: 2 miles
Walking time: 1½ hours
Dixville Notch, New Hampshire

DIXVILLE NOTCH, ALTHOUGH ONLY 2.5 MILES
long, offers some of the best scenery in New Hampshire, along with
the elegant Balsams Hotel Resort, which boasts a golf course, tennis
courts, swimming, boating, hiking, cross-country and downhill
skiing, and fabulous hospitality. It is also famous as the town that is
always the first to report its vote in national elections.

Flumes and picnic areas along NH 26 are worth a stop. Especially
prominent as you approach the notch from the west or leave it from
the east are great rocks of vertical strata that look more like western
landscapes than eastern mountains.

Forming the south of the notch, 2,780-foot Mount Gloriette includes
four rocky pinnacles: Third Cliff, Table Rock, Old King, and Profile
Cliff, which jut out from the north side of the mountain. It is to the
top of one of these formations that this walk will take you. Table
Rock has been a well-known climb for generations of visitors to the
Balsams. It's well worth its strenuous first part.

ACCESS

Dixville Notch is about 45 miles from Lancaster, north on US 3 to
Colebrook, and then 9 miles east on NH 26; or about 42 miles from
Berlin, north on NH 16 to NH 26, and then about 10 miles northwest
from there. Park in a small parking area on the south side of the road
just under the rock formations.

TRAIL

Your path enters the woods from the northeast corner of the parking
lot, and immediately takes you on a nearly vertical climb over slabs
of rock, which can be quite slippery when wet. Your compensation
is that when the rocks are wet, so are the balsam trees that hug the

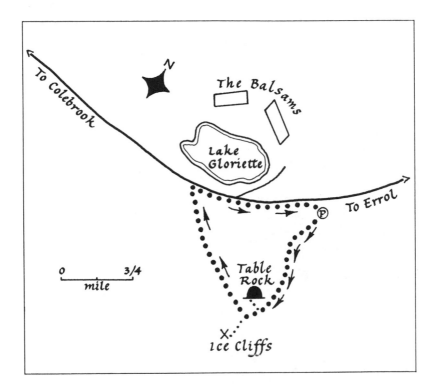

trail and smell like Christmas. A white-throated sparrow encourages you with its song as you begin to wonder if this walk is for you. Take heart. It is.

In about ten minutes you notice that you are now in birch woods, and in ten more you reach perpendicular, moss-covered, mammoth cliffs. Great roots stick out in places you might think you can't get up, to give you helpful handholds. Two more minutes and you see sky through the trees ahead; suddenly you're on flat ground at a junction.

Turn right to clamber up a small rise onto the rock, and walk out to views you'll be glad you came for. The "table" is less than ten feet wide at its narrowest, and extends 100 feet out over the notch. To your right you see the notch and towers of stone across the road on Mount Sanguinari. Look down to your left on the Balsams Hotel, where antlike people swim, play golf, paddle a party boat on Lake Gloriette.

A great root makes a helpful handhold.

When you've enjoyed the view and your lunch and a rest from the climb, go back to the junction where you turned right. There are clear signs on a tree directing you to NH 26 via a gentler path down, which goes behind the summit of Mount Gloriette.

From the junction climb uphill, past the bunchberry plants and through ferns and wood sorrel, to signs that point right (west). You will also see a sign for the ice cliffs, a small gorge which usually has ice in it year round. It's an interesting detour of about five minutes, including enjoyment time.

Back at the trail signs, your way is clearly marked with blue blazes on trees. You cross a ridge and then go gradually downhill. In about ten minutes you cross a brook on a birch-log bridge. You'll leave the brook for about fifteen minutes to descend a couple of steeper drops through the hardwood forest. Then you come to the brook and cross it again before another fairly steep drop, the sound of cars, and a glimpse of the road.

At the bottom, turn right on a cross-country ski trail marked "8," and follow it to the road. Turn right and walk .5 mile (carefully—traffic is swift here and the road curves) along Lake Gloriette, past the Dixville Notch Information Booth, and slightly uphill to your car.

4. Brunswick Springs

Walking distance: 1 mile
Walking time: 1–2 hours
Brunswick Springs, Vermont

ONE-HALF MILE DOWN AN UNMARKED DIRT ROAD, sixty-five feet above the Connecticut River and twenty feet below its steep bank, you will find six pools. Each is said to contain a different mineral with its own curative powers: iron, calcium, magnesium, sulphur, bromine, and arsenic. You'll smell the sulphur as you approach the pools. The water, cold and effervescent, pours from six pipes built into the bank.

The springs have been called the eighth wonder of the world. The Abenaki Indians claimed that curative powers embodied the waters they called Nebisonbik (Mineral Water Place). The Abenaki were also reputed to have placed a curse on anyone who used the waters for commercial purposes. Many legends have grown up around the springs, persuading people that the waters would cure all manner of diseases.

The first white man to visit the springs was a British soldier captured by the Indians during the French and Indian Wars. A medicine man helped to restore the soldier's wounded arm to full use by holding it under streams of water from the springs. Not long after that white settlers came to the region. From 1790 to 1860 residents on both sides of the river took in boarders who sought the mineral cures, and the springs eventually became famous. Entrepreneurs built a hotel near them and installed pipes from the pools to facilitate collection of the waters, which were bottled and sold. Within a few years the hotel burned. Then a small lodge was built on the hill above the springs. It was operated from 1910 to 1929, when it, too, burned. A new hotel was begun, but burned before completion. The Abenaki curse?

Twenty-five thousand people a year visited this area during its prime to take advantage of the powers of the springs, and many claimed to be cured. One man, who in 1945 had back trouble that doctors couldn't help, began to drink a blend of the waters. His back troubles disappeared completely. Of course, there are no scientifically proven claims

20

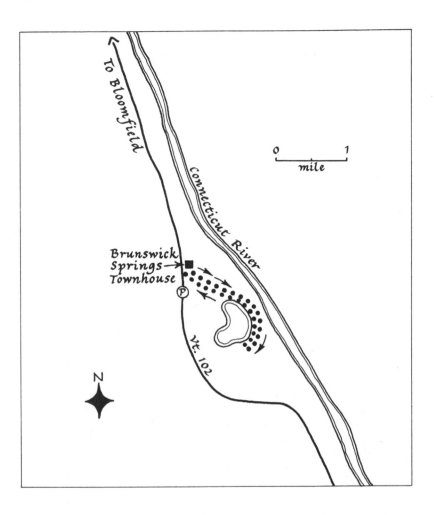

for the health-giving powers of the springs, and chemical analysis has indicated that there is no significant difference in the mineral content from one spring to another. Who do we believe?

A stroll down the dirt road to the springs will renew you, even if the springs won't. You can see some of nature's miracles: lilies on the pond; a pair of colorful wood ducks paddling into a colony of reeds.

ACCESS

From Bloomfield, Vermont, just across the bridge from North Stratford, New Hampshire that crosses the Connecticut River, turn south onto VT 102 and travel for about 2 miles. You'll see the Brunswick Springs Town House on your left. There's an unmarked dirt road just past the Town House and room to park your car.

TRAIL

Walk down the road, past the pine woods and a lily-filled pond on your right, to a bend in the road. On your left is an opening which, you will discover, is part of the Connecticut River's bank. Cement steps lead down to the pools that collect the spring waters.

After you've explored the springs and the old hotel foundations, and gazed down on the river, continue your walk along the dirt road beside the pond, or eat your lunch at the pond's edge. This road would be nice to ski on in the winter.

Cold and effervescent water tumbles from six pipes into six pools.

5. Percy Peaks

Walking distance: 3½ miles
Walking time: 4 hours
Stratford and Groveton, New Hampshire

THE ALMOST TWIN PERCY PEAKS DOMINATE MUCH
of the landscape in the vicinity of Groveton, as well as the land eastward from the other side of the Connecticut River as you drive south
along VT 102. The taller north peak has an open summit with magnificent views and, in season, fat blueberries to reward you for a
relatively tough climb. The south peak is heavily wooded and has no
trails.

ACCESS

Drive 2.6 miles east of Groveton on NH 110 and turn north onto
Emerson Road. It's 2.2 miles to Emerson School Corner, the beginning of Nash Stream Road. Follow this road 2.8 miles northward
along Nash Stream until you see a large rock on the right. A few feet
beyond the rock there's a small opening into the woods, usually
marked by an orange ribbon on a branch.

TRAIL

Inside the opening, beyond the orange streamer, there's a small cairn
of rocks and an old sign. The trail immediately turns right over some
stepping stones and then starts uphill along a cascading brook. In late
summer the hobblebush leaves turn purple; its berries are red. The
maples have already begun to turn, and an occasional red leaf drops
to the path you walk. Pink berries weight the stems of false Solomon's
seal. Sun shines through the spruces and lights the birches and
beeches, whose leaves will soon turn yellow.

An arrow on a brown sign directs you to the right after about ten
minutes. You cross a small brook and the path becomes more level.
Across Slide Brook, logging trucks gun their motors, and slashed limbs
on the ground give evidence of recent logging. Do those splashes of

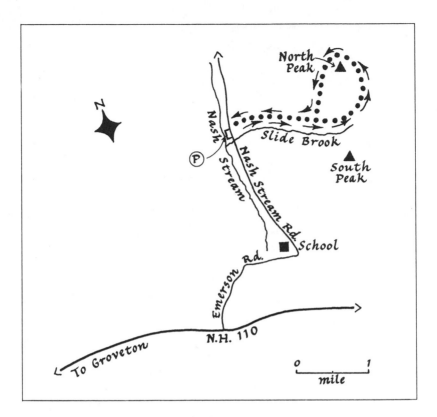

blue paint on certain trees mean that they will soon be cut, or that they are to be left for posterity to enjoy?

The trail bears left around birch trees growing on enormous rocks, and up a small rise from which you can look down on the brook. Club mosses stand straight up from the forest floor. There aren't many blazes, but the trail is distinct. The woods feel so wild that the modern screech and rumble of the trucks seems incredible. Your path is now a brook bed that runs east-southeast toward a tremendous boulder covered with rock tripe and moss. Pass under a tree that bridges the path there and continue southeast to climb above the brook again. A towering yellow birch could surely win the state contest for the biggest tree of its kind.

The trail moves steeply uphill as it leaves the brook. The woods are entirely large white birches now, although one of them wears a

24

yellow birch wrapped around its trunk. You come to what the Percys are famous for—great slabs of slippery granite. Follow blazes to the right. Five minutes later a wide view opens up westward to Vermont hills. Walk up over eroded roots (and sometimes wet rocks—take care) to a stone bench on one of the granite slabs. A sign overhead says, "Slab Trail to North Percy." It's time to sit on the bench, enjoy the view, a snack, and a well-earned drink from your water bottle.

Do not take the Slab Trail. It's usually very slippery. A pile of bleached bones at the bottom of the slab suggest the demise of a young moose who took the wrong step here and probably fell to its death. Face the mountain and bear right to a trail marked by bright yellow blazes. The woods emanate the scent of young balsam trees along the moss-covered path. Red spruces mingle with the balsams. The south peak rises on your right. The trail turns left up more slippery slabs (roots make good handholds), then winds through beech and birch forest up a sometimes rock-strewn path, through ferns, mosses, and wildflowers in springtime. Walk up a long, mossy granite ledge, along the trail again, left through a narrow passage between more moss-

Twin peaks almost dominate the northern landscape.

covered granite, and then left again along another long ledge. You soon come to your first view south to the Presidential Range, the Carters, Carter Notch, and the Mahoosuc Range.

Follow blazes along the ridge. Bunchberry, blueberries, and reindeer lichen grow along the path; cupped lactaria mushrooms hold last night's rain.

You're nearing the summit. The spruces reach up only waist-high. In ten minutes you're out in the sun again. Climb the steep rocks and bear right to follow rock cairns up, up, up over the ledges, through the blueberry bushes and out to the wide-open summit. From west to east you see the Nash Stream mountains, Sugarloaf, the little knob of Cape Horn, then the Franconias, the smokestacks of the Groveton paper mills, and the Upper Ammonoosuc River. Behind the river, North and South Twin rise on the horizon, and then you see the Presidentials again, along with the Carters and the Mahoosucs in a circle all around you.

Ravens overhead greet you. The blueberry bushes have turned their autumn red. As you lie on the sun-warmed summit rocks and rest from your strenuous climb, a bald eagle soars overhead—if you're lucky.

Be careful to follow the blazes and orange ribbons as you return the way you came, especially where you go through the narrow opening in the rocks. You turned left at these rocks to come up. Be sure to turn right on the way down.

6. Maidstone State Park

Walking distance: 1 mile
Walking time: about 1 hour
Between Bloomfield and Guildhall, Vermont

OVERDEVELOPMENT IN NORTHERN NEW ENGLAND alarms those who realize the need to preserve our last remaining open spaces for future generations. Rural ambiance, wildlife habitats, and recreational opportunities have already been destroyed in some parts. Lumber companies can no longer afford to keep thousands of acres of land that now go to the highest bidder. Proposals have been made to set aside much of this threatened land for national parks. Some people feel that such parks would not only save the land from ruin, but would also produce jobs in low-income areas.

Vermont's Northeast Kingdom National Park is one of those proposed. It would encompass some of the coldest, most remote, least inhabited counties in the state. This area boasts the highest concentration of lakes and ponds in Vermont, including some of the least developed ones.

Maidstone Lake lies in this region and could be part of the proposed national park. There is presently a state park on its shore. A walk through the park's quiet woods will give you a taste of what would be preserved for you and your descendants in Northeast Kingdom National Park.

ACCESS

Vermont 102 runs along the Connecticut River. Drive on it until you're approximately 5 miles south of Bloomfield, or approximately 10 miles north of Groveton, New Hampshire, or Guildhall, Vermont. You'll see a dirt road with a sign that directs you to Maidstone Lake and the state park. Drive 5 miles on the park road to the Ranger Contact Station, where you can park. There is a small admission fee, and you can request a trail map. The walk described here includes the Loon Trail and also the Shore Trail, which will return you to the Contact Station.

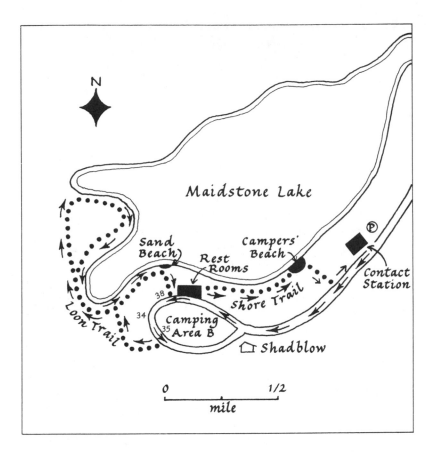

TRAIL

From the Contact Station walk to Camping Area B. A lean-to named "Shadblow" is on your left. Turn right downhill and follow a circle around to Campsites 34 and 35 and a sign for the Loon Trail. Turn right onto the trail and follow blue blazes on trees through maple woods and hobblebush, beeches and birches, many varieties of ferns, and moss-covered boulders. Club moss stands tall on the ground. You'll see clintonia's yellow bells in the spring, and its bright blue berries on long straight stems in the fall.

In about seven minutes you go down a long hill toward the lake, which shows through the trees. Turn left here to walk through birch woods. Notice the beaver lodge on the shore. The trail is narrow as

28

A tree grows over a split rock on the Shore Trail.

it runs along the water. In ten more minutes you cross a log bridge and the trail curves right. Another five minutes of walking brings you to a large fallen birch with a blue-and-white-striped ribbon tied around it.

Climb over the birch to go uphill and through a forest of towering spruces and new, bright green little ones that hug the side of the trail. The path makes a loop down a cove. Soon you see water on both sides of you. Circle around to the right and start back along the shore of the cove. There are lunch rocks at the water's edge. Goldthread carpets the ground. The trees on this side are mostly cedar. Their twisted trunks look as though someone had wrung them out to dry. Watch your step—there seem to be quite a few holes waiting to trap a foot.

Soon you reach a fallen spruce and another striped ribbon. Just beyond it is the birch you climbed over where you began the loop. Walk back to where you turned left onto the trail along the shore. Continue straight here to where the trail ends at a tiny sand beach. Go uphill to Campsite 38, turn left onto the road, and walk past the restrooms. When you see signs to the Shore Trail, cross the grass and find the trail just past some raspberry bushes.

The path is narrow and eroded, but close to the water again. Be careful to avoid slippery roots. You're in a forest of cedars and birches. The lake laps the shore beside you; tiny spruces create a miniature forest for you to walk through; brown mushrooms nestle beneath the trees. The trail ends at the campers' beach, where you can refresh your weary feet with a wade in the cool lake. Then go uphill to the road and turn left to reach your car fairly quickly.

7. Kettle Pond

Walking distance: 3.3 miles
Walking time: 2½ hours
Groton State Forest—Groton, Vermont

GROTON STATE FOREST, AMID SCENIC VERMONT hills, is the largest single piece of property owned by the state. It encompasses over 25,000 acres of land, and overlaps into five towns in the center of Vermont. Its ponds form the headwaters of the Wells River. Within the forest are campgrounds, picnic areas, lakes and ponds, bridle and hiking trails, and multi-use trails for year-round recreation. Primitive camping is allowed with permission.

The forest has a long history. Ice Age glaciers polished the mountain peaks, leaving sand, rocks, and boulders behind as they melted; low-lying places became ponds, lakes, and streams. Abenaki Indians camped and hunted here long before the white man arrived. During the French and Indian Wars in the early 1700s, Indian hunting bands and French and English raiding parties passed through. The area's network of ponds, brooks, and rivers was used by the French and the Indians to carry captives of the infamous Deerfield, Massachusetts massacre north to Canada.

After the American Revolution settlers came to farm nearby and to cut the trees of the forest for fuel, lumber, and the manufacture of potash. Logging became the main industry, and is still important today. The Wells and Connecticut Rivers provided good access to the forest from the rest of New England. In the late 1800s railroads came and carried Groton Forest's lumber to places where it was sorely needed. For a long time these trains were the major mode of transportation to the forest ponds and the saw mills that operated on them. The trains themselves used up a tremendous amount of wood for fuel.

Railroads opened the forest to seasonal campers as early as 1894. Local Vermonters came in the summer to camp, and again in the fall to hunt. Trains dropped them off at Lakeside Station or Rocky Point Flag Stop, and from these stops they took boats to their cabins on the shores of Groton Pond.

31

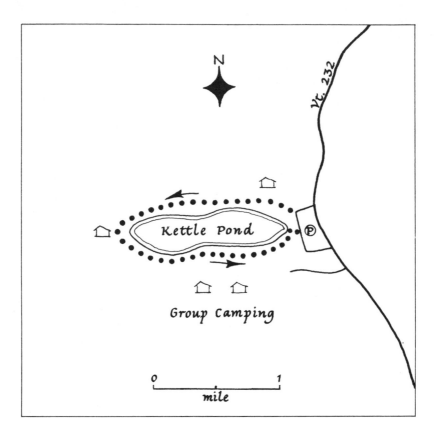

In 1919 the state began to buy the land that now comprises the State Forest. The 1930s saw the Civilian Conservation Corps help to develop the main forest road, the campgrounds, and the park in general. Today, the Department of Forests, Parks, and Recreation, with the public's cooperation, protects the valuable resources here, which include timber, fish, wildlife, plant life, and clean water, so that we may use and enjoy them forever.

The walk described here circles Kettle Pond. Legend says that in the mid-1800s Bristol Bill, renowned counterfeiter and bankrobber, buried a kettle of counterfeit bills beside the pond. He was captured in Groton and brought to trial in Danville, where he stabbed the prosecuting attorney with a case knife.

ACCESS

Take VT 232, either north from US 302 at Groton, or south from US 2 just before Marshfield, 18 miles west of St. Johnsbury and 16 miles east of Montpelier. Excellent signs direct you to the Forest, and then on to the Kettle Pond Parking Area—on the right if you're driving south, on the left if you're driving north.

TRAIL

The trail, marked frequently by blue blazes on trees, begins at the northwest corner of the parking lot. It is narrow at first. Just before you reach the pond it turns right into a birch forest. There's an Adirondack shelter uphill on your right, and an outhouse on your right a little farther along.

After an early October snowfall the leaves scattered on the ground are blanketed in white, as are the slippery roots beneath them—be careful as you walk. The trail soon leads you down to the pond, which is edged with leatherleaf and sweet gale bushes. Great grey rocks look like dolphins humping their backs in the shallows; wood ducks dive for lunch far out on the water. Blueberry leaves and sumac make a red border around the shore. There are many openings along the lakeside path with nice rocks to sit upon and views to enjoy.

In about half a mile the blue arrows lead you to your right away from the pond, and then almost immediately two blue arrows on a tree tell you to turn left, into hemlock woods. The path is smoother now. The new snow dampens the balsams, and their pungent odor permeates the woods. In springtime sheep laurel and labrador tea blossoms decorate this part of the pond. Wintergreen grows along the path. There's a broken-down beaver lodge on the water's edge. Red-breasted nuthatches and chickadees tell you that winter has come early this year. You pass a fireplace in a clearing that was once a campsite. Bright red bunchberries peek at you from a hole between two rocks. The forest looks older now. There's a house opposite you, across the lake. You're a bit over a mile down the trail when you come to another Adirondack shelter, this one with a fireplace. It makes a great refreshment stop on a snowy day. If the shelters on this walk tempt you to stay overnight sometimes, get camping information from the Department of Forests, Parks, and Recreation, 103 South Main Street, Waterbury, VT 05676, or from the Forest Supervisor at Groton State Forest during the summer season.

Looking at Kettle Pond from Owl's Head.

From here the trail takes on quite a different character. There are some wet areas, and you walk mostly over moss-covered rocks. You're at the end of the pond. Large red paint blazes on trees indicate a boundary. Stay with the blue blazes and walk around the end of the lake. You'll see lots of big boulders, many prettily covered with polypody ferns. Pines stand between you and the shore here. You're not as close to the water as you were on the other side. About .3 mile farther brings you to the house you saw from the other shore. The path smooths a little and then becomes rocky and mossy again. You reach more mixed hardwoods, their autumn colors brightening the forest to either side of you, and you arrive at several shelters that are the group camping area.

Continue out onto a wide road and turn toward the lake. Just before the shore a narrow trail leads to the right, through bramble bushes and rhododendron, and across a log bridge. Turn right when you come to a wide path, which soon narrows and leads you in about five minutes to your car.

34

8. Bretzfelder Memorial Park—Four Seasons Trail

Walking distance: 1 mile
Walking time: 1 hour
Bethlehem, New Hampshire

IN 1979 HELEN BRETZFELDER BEQUEATHED SEV-
enteen acres of land to the Society for the Protection of New Hampshire Forests, to be used as a public park and conservancy for the
Town of Bethlehem. The Society has added a demonstration forest.
School children of Bethlehem have cut the Four Seasons Trail through
the demonstration forest, and have written a guide to the trail to
educate both the adults and the children who visit the park. As are
all properties of the Society, the park is open to the public with the
hope that it will be enjoyed and respected as an ecological and recreational treasure. Hiking trails, fishing spots, picnic tables, and cross-
country ski trails are available. All are welcome to birdwatch, enjoy
the flowers, and learn about the forest. Stop at the little house at the
edge of the parking lot to inquire about the many summer programs
offered by the Society.

ACCESS

In the village of Bethlehem, next to the golf course, find Prospect
Street off Main Street (NH 302). Drive north on Prospect Street for
1 mile. A large sign on the left marks the entrance to the park and
one of its two parking lots.

TRAIL

There's a sign that says "Nature Trail" in the north corner of the
parking lot. Follow the trail into a sweet smelling balsam woods.
There's cinnamon fern on the forest floor and an occasional foam
flower in June. You'll come to the first of several explanatory tablets.
This one tells you about the many uses of pine trees. They create

35

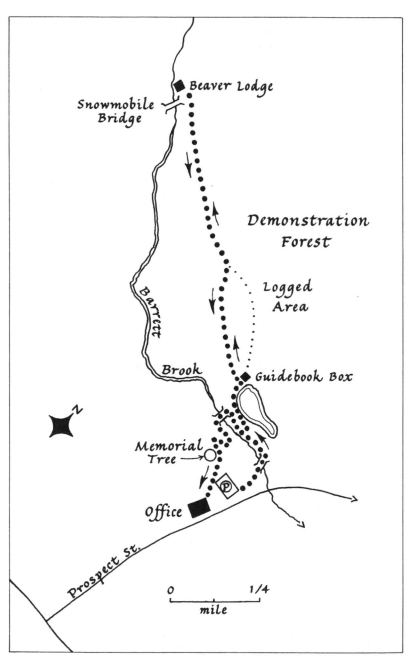

Beaver Lodge

Snowmobile
Bridge

Demonstration
Forest

Logged
Area

Barrett

Brook

Guidebook Box

N

Memorial
Tree

P

Office

Prospect St.

0   1/4
              mile

homes and feeding grounds for woodpeckers, shade from hot summer sun for animals and humans, and are used to construct sturdy furniture. Their roots hold the soil from eroding, and their seeds create future forests.

Cross the little wooden bridge that spans the brook. Local wildlife depends on the purity of this water. You might see or catch a trout, or you might see a small boy sitting high up on a glacial erratic boulder, dangling his line in hopes of a catch. The trail bears right, past another informative plaque, and soon reaches a small pond with picnic tables beside it. There are fish to be caught here, too.

Walk along the pond's edge to its northwest corner. There's a box here that contains guidebooks for you to borrow. Numbered signs on the trees from here on correspond with descriptions in the guidebook.

The Four Seasons Trail through the demonstration forest begins just ahead of you, and then leads you up a long hill through the woods, past a lush growth of beech ferns, and into a cleared area. You'll soon go downhill through a logged area. Turn right at the appropriate sign to return to the pond. To see the rest of the forest, turn left onto the skid road, where downed trees were "skidded" through the forest to logging trucks that hauled them away. You'll see slash piles, left here so that they will return nutrients to the soil and provide nesting places for chipmunks and winter wrens. Much of the slash from this cut was chipped and sold to a wood-burning power plant.

Patches of bunchberry flowers bloom along the road in May. They'll produce red berries to tell you when summer is almost at an end. Watch for lady's slipper and the small toads that may hop in front of you. In June there will be wild strawberries, and in July, raspberries. The open woods around you are home to deer, but chances of seeing one are rare—they hide too well. The red ribbons on trees mark new ski trails.

Black cherry trees have been deliberately left to provide food for wildlife. Young birches and balsam firs have been left to produce a future timber crop. The latest harvest was taken in the winter while the ground and the brooks were frozen, in order to minimize erosion problems. The harvest was planned both for immediate profit and to increase the timber and recreational values of the area.

Between signs 13 and 14 there's a hardy growth of new trees. At 14 you can bear left to the snowmobile bridge over the brook to see the abandoned beaver lodge. Weather and high water have just about

You might see a small boy dangling his line in hopes of a catch.

collapsed this lodge, but it looks as though the beavers had decided to move on anyway.

Now go back the way you came, past the pond. Please return the guidebook to the box for the next person who needs it. Turn right, away from the pond and into the woods again. When you reach the brook turn right at the Loop Trail sign, and follow that trail across another wooden bridge and up a steep hill. Turn left at the top of the hill. Be sure to look down at the cascading brook below you, and to catch a glimpse of the pond through the trees beyond. Continue past the Memorial Tree and back to your car.

Although Forest Society properties are open to the public free of charge, donations for their support are gratefully received. The work of the Society is vital to the future of all of us. You can join the Society and receive bulletins regarding this important work and the opportunity to take part in it personally. Write to The Society for the Protection of New Hampshire Forests, 54 Portsmouth Street, Concord, New Hampshire 03301, or stop in at the office at Bretzfelder Memorial Park for information on how you can help.

9. Red Barns Trail

Walking distance: ½ mile
Walking time: 45 minutes
Bethlehem, New Hampshire

THE RED BARNS TRAIL IS PART OF THE ROCKS ES-
tate, built in 1882 by John Jacob Glessner, a Chicago businessman.
The Estate, one of many mountain summer homes built by city people
in the years following the Civil War, provided an escape to cool mountain air and magnificent scenery.

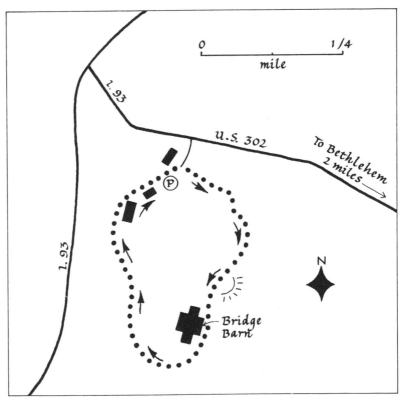

Boulders left behind by the melting glaciers of the Ice Age gave the Rocks Estate its name. Some of the boulders still lie in the fields, and many inhabit the woods now used as an activity center for the Society for the Protection of New Hampshire Forests. Over 1,200 acres of woodlands, including a large Christmas tree plantation and fields for haying, are managed by the Society. Educational programs for all ages take place here throughout the year and are open to the public, as are the trails for cross-country skiers.

The Red Barns Wayside Area and self-guiding nature trail, about .5 mile west of the main entrance to the estate, was once the farm of Hosea Crane. The little red house was later the home of Charles Brown, for forty-six years a beloved superintendent of the Rocks. The Nature Trail teaches us a lot about farm life in the North Country, the mountains, woodland flowers and trees, and the conservation of land for posterity.

ACCESS

From I-93 take Exit 40 east, toward Bethlehem. Almost immediately on your right is the Society for the Preservation of New Hampshire Forests sign, and a driveway leading up past a red, Cape Cod–style house and around to your left to a parking area for the Red Barns Trail. There are explanatory folders in a box attached to an informational sign across the parking lot, at the trailhead.

TRAIL

Cross the old stone wall ahead of you and to the left of the sign, and walk through a forest that grew up on what was once pasture. Early New Hampshire farmers had great difficulty clearing the land of rocks and boulders left by the glaciers. Some farmers just gave up and let the forest reclaim the land.

In the spring and early summer many varieties of wildflowers decorate your trail. At the top of the hill look beyond the stone wall over vast fields to a panorama of the mountains. Then follow the path to an old wagon wheel overgrown with clematis. Blackberries, fir, and birch trees fill what used to be a clearing. A woodshed and farm machinery once occupied this space.

Soon you reach the unusual bridge barn. Horses, cows, sheep, and pigs were raised at the Rocks. They required large quantities of hay,

40

so the barn was built to store hay from nearby fields. Horses pulled large hay wagons across the bridge onto a platform that runs the length of the barn. Hay was tossed into the storage area below, and the horses continued out the far door to draw their emptied wagons back to the fields for the next load.

Continue around the barn and down an old road known as the Pony Path. Long ago children rode their pony carts through the woods and into the fields to collect flowers for daisy chains, or bits of wood for carving. The trail, marked by an arrow, turns sharply right through the forest. Delicate ferns soften the forest floor where fallen branches and dead trees slowly decay, returning nutrients to the soil. Sometimes you can hear birds, and you may see moose tracks. The trail goes along an avenue lined with white birches. The paper birch has been used to make Indian canoes, paper, and firewood. These trees are handsome, especially when their yellow leaves light up the autumn woods.

All too soon your path turns right and you walk along another wall, pass another red barn, and return to your car.

The bridge barn.

10. Autumn Wildflowers at Scotland Brook

Walking distance: about 1½ miles
Walking time: about 2 hours, depending on your curiosity
Landaff, New Hampshire

THE SCOTLAND BROOK SANCTUARY OF THE AU-dubon Society of New Hampshire was dedicated in the winter of 1985–86 at a ceremony that took place in the snow. The sanctuary is comprised of 102 acres of varied terrain and animal habitats, with walking trails in varying states of repair—dependent on the help of some conscientious volunteers.

There are hardwood and softwood forests, here, a beaver pond, and lots of birds and wildflowers. Wood duck, bear, deer, moose, and beaver inhabit the sanctuary. The area is particularly well known among flower lovers for its ten species of wild orchids, which usually bloom in July. There are at least five species of asters and many kinds of goldenrod, as well as other autumn flowers, and the berries that replace spring blossoms in the fall.

Settlers from Scotland and Ireland farmed here and raised sheep a century ago. Stone walls through the forest give evidence of former pasture boundaries. Today the Audubon Society manages the plantation of spruce and balsam trees by careful, selective cutting for Christmas trees that are sold to the public. The profits benefit the Audubon Society.

These woods are open for walks and cross-country skiing. The Audubon Society schedules informative exploratory trips here at various times of the year. You can learn more about these tours if you write or call The Audubon Society of New Hampshire, P.O. Box 528-B, Concord, New Hampshire, 03302. Telephone: 603-224-9909.

Nature guidebooks will enhance your enjoyment of this walk.

ACCESS

From I-93 take Exit 17 for Franconia. Turn right onto NH 18 and

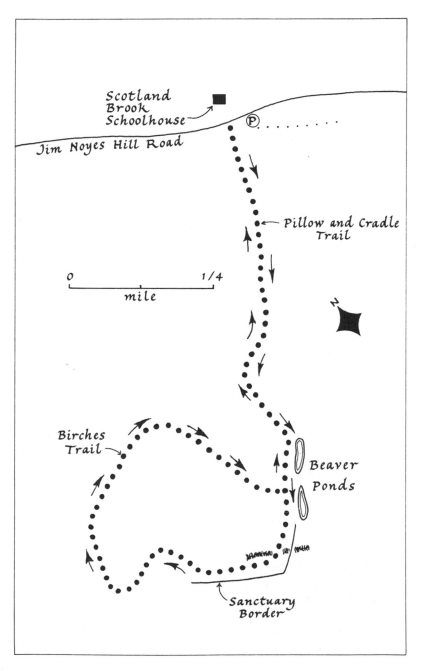

Scotland
Brook
Schoolhouse

Jim Noyes Hill Road

Pillow and Cradle
Trail

0   1/4
mile

Birches
Trail

Beaver
Ponds

Sanctuary
Border

N

drive north for just a minute to a junction with NH 117. Turn left onto NH 117. Where this road takes a hairpin turn to the right, you turn left onto Pearl Lake Road. Travel this paved road for 4 miles to a fork at the lake. Turn left and travel along the lakeshore for 2 miles to a junction with Jim Noyes Hill Road, which is gravel. Turn left and reach the old white schoolhouse in .3 mile. The sanctuary sign is on your right. Please do not park at the schoolhouse—it's private property. You may park in front of the sign or beside the road.

TRAIL

Your walk begins across the street from the schoolhouse, where a wide swath through the field makes a trail, edged in the fall by shoulder-high asters and goldenrod. The trail enters the woods. Many varieties of mushrooms pop out of the soggy forest floor. Turkeytail fungus (easily recognized by its shape—little turkey tails about 2 inches across) hugs fallen logs. You wander along the forest road. The last turtlehead blossom of the summer clings to its stem beside your path, which is long and straight through these woods, eventually bending to the right.

Deep green mosses and lots of wood sorrel cover the ground as the woods open up. The mixed forest is bright with autumn color. Little masked tree frogs hop in front of your feet. They're so well camouflaged that you can barely see them. There are deep blue berries on the clintonia that bore yellow bells in the spring; black berries hang from Indian cucumber root. If you want to see the round-leaved orchid, you must search for it at this time of year. Look for white lettuce, a tall-stemmed flower with creamy, whitish-green flowers. It is apt to bear as many as four different leaf shapes on one stem.

You really should bring a mushroom book on this walk, for you'll come across many varieties. It would be pointless to describe them here because the next time one appears in any given place, it may be of a different variety. Amateur mycologists should look, but not touch.

Now you reach the beaver pond. A bit farther along the path are the remains of an older pond and a tremendous abandoned beaver lodge close to the shore. Smartweed, skullcap, and nodding bur marigold bloom here.

There's a trail junction as you reach the end of the pond. Your way goes straight ahead to make a loop of about forty-five minutes walking, which will return you to the junction. Go up the side of a hill along

44

An abandoned beaver lodge close to the shore.

an old stone wall. In the spring lots of clintonia and violets bloom here. Christmas fern grows in abundance. The trail winds left, uphill, and through a break in another stone wall onto an old town road that you follow for a while. Don't miss the rattlesnake plantain that grows in your path. It has variegated green leaves and a tall-stemmed, creamy flower.

The road re-enters pine woods, and soon there's an arrow directing you into a right-hand turn. Go downhill to meet the skeleton of a sentinel pine, full of woodpecker holes now. It once stood in the middle of a farmer's field. Several kinds of club moss shelter the ground. Turn left when you reach the pond again. Follow the trail until you come out of the woods into the field of goldenrod and asters where you began your walk. You might be just in time to enjoy a mixed flock of warblers and chickadees stopping in a nearby maple tree for a rest on their way to somewhere. Come back in the winter to enjoy a day of skiing, and don't forget that the orchids bloom in July.

The Appalachian Trail and Nearby Gentle Hills

11. Black Mountain

Walking distance: 4.6 miles
Walking time: 2½ hours
Benton, New Hampshire

THE VIEWS FROM BLACK MOUNTAIN'S SUMMIT IN
all seasons, and the rhodora display below the summit in late May,
make this small mountain above the Connecticut River Valley a
favorite destination. Birdwatchers here catch glimpses of hawks and
ravens, warblers, and white-throated sparrows, and the chickadees
that feast on mountain ash berries as winter approaches.

ACCESS

Seven and four-tenths miles east of North Haverhill on NH 116 lies
the tiny village of Benton, and a junction where green signs point
south to the Haverhills. Turn right and drive .9 mile south to the last
house on the left, after which the pavement turns to dirt—you'll see
evidence of logging operations. If the weather has been particularly
wet, park here and walk the half mile to the trailhead. Usually the
road is driveable all the way to the brown-and-white sign marked "P"
for parking, and a small sign that reads, "Black Mountain Trail 2.3
miles."

TRAIL

Your route leads south on an old road through balsam, birch, and
poplar woods. Fall asters and Christmas fern decorate its banks. When
the trees are bare you can see through their branches to the valley
you've left behind. Soon you cross a field of goldenrod to a trail into
the woods and another brown sign, this one bearing the figure of a
hiker. A National Forest arrow directs you to the right. From here
on yellow oblong blazes on trees will guide you. There are a couple
of steep uphill walks, tempered with nearly level stretches. About half
an hour from your car you'll by-pass an overgrown clearcut area that
offers views north and west into the valley.

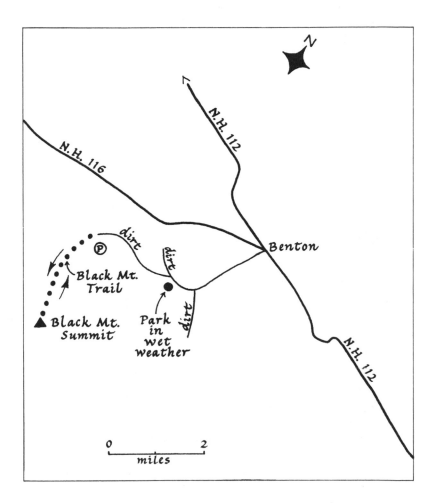

Continue uphill, southeast and then south, through fine open woods. Notice the tiny moose ears on the winter hobblebush to the right of the path. In late fall bits of ice form on a small brook that crosses your road. You reach another overgrown clearcut studded with hundreds of young trees, and walk over remnants of the corduroy road the loggers built.

You're about an hour from your car by the time you start uphill over a steep bank adorned with ferns. Next you cross a gentle ridge into the shelter of evergreens, and ascend a ledgy incline that soon levels out again. Rime ice crunches underfoot in November. Wet

Mount Moosilauke hides beneath clouds.

leaves pad the trail, and dustings of snow along its edges let you know that winter is on its way. The pungent smell of the bright green balsams along the path makes you dream of Christmas.

Sky shows through the trees, and another fifteen minutes of walking brings you to the summit. Walk up onto the magnificent quartzite ledges for a splendid view. Mount Moosilauke looms straight ahead behind Mount Clough. To your right, its ledges showing through the trees, stands Sugarloaf Mountain, and south of it, Blueberry Mountain, described in another walk in this book. The sharp outline of Owl's Head is south of Blueberry. Look south over the tranquil Connecticut River Valley, and westward to the tiny towns of North Haverhill in New Hampshire, and Newbury in Vermont. Far to the northeast are Mount Kinsman and the Franconias.

In spring take the Chippewa Trail, from its junction with your trail, down far enough to see the rhodora blooms, which usually appear during the last week of May or the first week of June. You may never forget their flashes of deep pink against the quartzite ledges of Black Mountain.

Return the way you came for an easy downhill ramble to your car.

12. Blueberry Mountain

Walking distance: 4 miles
Walking time: 3 hours
Benton, New Hampshire

BLUEBERRY IS ONE OF SEVERAL SMALL BUT SATIS-
fying mountains in the Connecticut River Valley, north of Hanover
and south of Littleton. It's in an especially pretty piece of the valley,
and the views you'll get with little effort are a prize at all seasons of
the year.

ACCESS

From NH 25 at Glencliff, west of Plymouth or east of Haverhill, drive
north from the Glencliff Church for 1 mile. There's a dirt road on
the left called North and South Road, opposite a white farmhouse.
You'll see Appalachian Trail signs and a sign warning you that the
road is not maintained in the winter. Turn left onto North and South
Road. Travel .7 mile, past the Tunnel Brook Trail sign on your right,
and up a long hill to the Blueberry Mountain Trail sign on your left.
Turn left into an ample parking area.

TRAIL

The easy walk begins as an old logging or town road through beech
woods. Behind the woods is evidence of logging, and there's much
slash left on the ground by the loggers. Owl's Head appears in back
of the slash. Clover growing in the road suggests that this was probably
once pasture, and an overgrown cellar hole on the left says that someone once lived here.

In about twenty minutes you'll come to a fireplace, and a sign
indicating a trail on your left, where you see a yellow blaze on a tree.
Follow the yellow blazes to the summit.

A great clump of pewter-colored beeches and white birches stand
silhouetted against the sharp blue sky. The road bears around to the
right. Several paths lead away from the road, but don't take them.

51

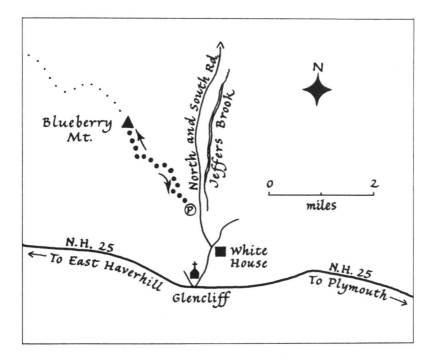

Survey stakes have recently appeared along the road, and we shudder to think of another condominium village. Maybe it won't ever be built.

In April you'll be anxious for spring flowers. Chances are, just when you've decided you're a bit early, tiny yellow violets will appear to decorate your path, even though patches of snow still dapple the forest floor. The snow-capped ridge of Mount Moosilauke appears. You pass some great boulders. A trailside beech with a heart-shaped blister has "DM 70 RAW" carved on its trunk. The beeches are larger here. It's a fine, open forest. You see evidence of other romantic couples who strolled here. Marianna and Gabriel left their names on one of the beeches, too. The pink and white blossoms of spring beauty interrupt the trail, and adder's tongue leaves promise blooms to come. Lots of trailing arbutus, but no buds yet. An abundance of sheep laurel will be pink in June.

A red pine forest begins now, and you come out onto granite ledges with views of Mount Moosilauke, Mount Clough, Hurricane Mountain, and the gentler hills of the Connecticut Valley. There are stone

52

cairns to direct you, and then a yellow blaze leads you into some evergreen woods on your right. Up here in the sun you will see buds on the arbutus, and later, fragrant open blossoms.

About ten minutes of walking brings you to a larger cairn with a post sticking out of it. One supposes that this is technically the summit, but off to the right and through the woods are more ledges that seem to be at higher elevation. If you're curious and careful, walk across a swampy, mossy area and up over the rocks, eastward toward Mount Moosilauke, until you come to some flat-topped ledges with cairns on them. Two stacks of small rocks, about 500 feet apart, offer no indication of any further trail or of why the stacks of rocks are there. Anyway, it's a nice place to lunch, and you do get a view of Black Mountain's white ledges and a glimpse of the farmed valley below.

The trip back gives you time to look for the downy woodpecker who hammers somewhere nearby, and to see the flicker dash off through the treetops. Notice the coltsfoot blossoms that have burst into bloom while you lunched in the noonday sun up top.

Jeffers Brook cascades through a deep gorge across the road from where you parked. The Tunnel Brook Trail, a good walk or ski tour, is described in Daniel Doan's *50 More Hikes in New Hampshire* (Backcountry Publications) in his walk to Mud Pond. He also describes Black Mountain's Chippewa Trail. For other hikes in the vicinity, see the Appalachian Mountain Club's *White Mountains Guide*. Black Mountain's Black Mountain Trail is elsewhere in this book.

13. The Palisades

Walking distance: 1½ miles
Walking time: 1¼ hours
Fairlee, Vermont

IF YOU'RE DRIVING ON I-91 OR VT 5 THROUGH VER-
mont or NH 10 on the other side of the Connecticut River, you can't
help but notice the perpendicular cliffs that rise above the river at
Fairlee. They're called the Palisades. The view from the top of these
cliffs is one of the nicest to be found along the river. The walk up is
steep, but takes little time and is worth the effort. New Hampshire
hills and mountains, farms, and the magnificent village of Orford
across the river from Fairlee comprise the scenery you'll see from atop
the Palisades. It was from Orford that Samuel Morey, in the spring
of 1793, launched his now famous steamboat. This was the first time
steam had been applied to paddlewheels to propel a boat. The Morey
home is one of those handsome white houses that line the main street
of Orford.

Fairlee, on the Vermont shore of the Connecticut, is well known
for its Aloha Camps, an offshoot of which is The Hulbert Outdoor
Center. The people there specialize in year-round outdoor education
programs for school and adult groups. They welcome you to the big
white house at the north end of the lake, where you can get local
hiking hints and learn about the center's exceptional programs.

Also well worth a visit in Fairlee is Chapman's Store, which has
been owned and run by the same family for three generations. The
Chapmans are a friendly lot, and they carry a most amazing variety
of goods in their store.

ACCESS

From VT 5, or the I-91 exit at Fairlee, take the road west toward
Lake Morey. Then take your first right-hand turn. You will see an
old, shingled building (used for maintenance purposes in the summer
and boarded up in the off-season) with "Lake Morey" written on its
roof. You can park here for your walk.

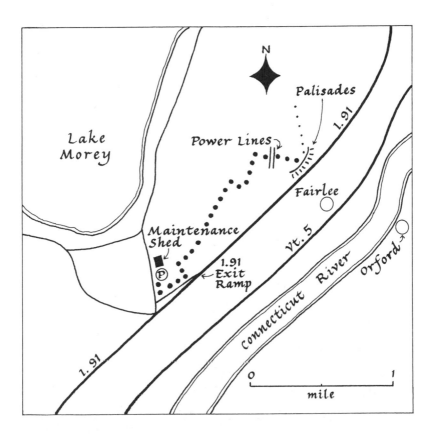

TRAIL

From the building mentioned above, walk southward, across the grass and toward the highway, until you come to a chain fence. Go around the fence, turning left onto a well-worn path that runs northeast. The exit ramp from I-91 is on your right, and a row of splendid red pines stands to your left. At the end of the row of pines, a narrow trail leads uphill into the woods. Look for the yellow trail marker of the Lake Morey Association on a tree where you enter. You'll follow these yellow markers to the summit.

The first part of the trail goes steeply uphill. Eastward are views of Mount Cube behind a smaller, cone-shaped mountain; Smarts Mountain rises a bit south of Cube. Both are in New Hampshire.

The river runs past Orford across from Fairlee.

White pines, hemlock, and lots of oaks form the forest here. You'll get glimpses of Lake Morey and the hills behind it as you go.

Soon you come to a hole in the fence. Go through the hole and continue northward up another long hill. If you look at your feet when the going gets steep, the trail will seem to level out for you.

In about fifteen minutes there are good views of Lake Morey, and the trail really does level out. Be sure to keep an eye out for the markers. Ten more minutes and you climb over a fallen log. The trail leads to the right around some ledges, north again along a level stretch, then eastward, downhill, and across a log bridge over a brook that may be dry in summer. Now you're under the power lines, and there's a great open space with fine views of Fairlee, the south end of Orford, the river, and ribbonlike roads to either side of it.

Cross the clearing from west to east and find a yellow marker where the trail enters the woods again. Shiny wintergreen leaves decorate the ground beside your path, which winds around some granite ledges and then goes eastward along a level ridge to reach the open summit. If you sit in the right spot you can block out the highway and enjoy a view of the farmland, and the church spires, and the little white New England houses along the wide river at Orford.

Return the way you came.

14. Mount Cube

Walking distance: 7.8 miles
Walking time: 6 hours
Orford, New Hampshire

THE WALK TO THE OPEN SUMMITS OF MOUNT CUBE
is a real hike and requires sturdy boots or shoes, a sweater, water, lunch, and a rain- or windproof jacket. You should also carry a map and compass. A USGS or Appalachian Trail map of the area will help you identify what you see from the top. The trail is on a reroute of the Appalachian Trail, through some overgrown farmland. You pass old stone walls and farm roads through the woods to unusual rock formations at the summits. There are fine views of the Connecticut River Valley and its surrounding mountains.

ACCESS

From Hanover travel north 17.2 miles along the Connecticut River, via NH 10, to a junction with NH 25A. Turn right onto NH 25A and travel about 8.5 miles to an orange sign, on the right-hand side of the road, for the Appalachian Trail. This is just across from the athletic field of a summer camp. There's a small parking space for one car just west of the trail sign. The road's shoulders are fairly wide and will accommodate other cars.

If you travel on I-93, exit at Plymouth and drive northwest on NH 25 through Wentworth to NH 25A. Turn left onto NH 25A, drive 6 miles to the same trail sign, and park just beyond it.

TRAIL

The trail immediately leads you south, past purple asters and orange jewelweed, as tall as your shoulders by early September. Blue jays chatter as you cross the brook past a couple of large boulders (probably left here by melting glaciers) and continue into the hardwood forest. In early September the leaves are just on the edge of turning, and sunlight dances through them onto beech ferns below. In about fifteen

58

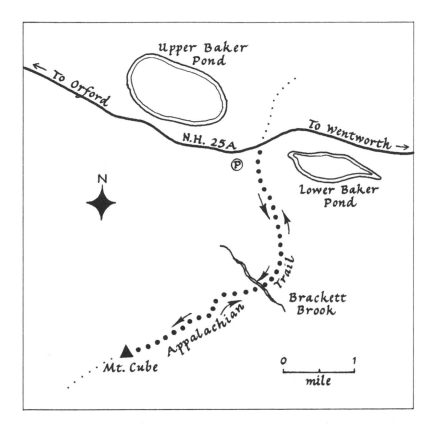

minutes you reach an old cellar hole on your right. Did someone leave here for more fertile western farmland, or move to the city during the Industrial Revolution?

You'll be treated to a display of heavenly blue, closed gentian flowers on either side of the path, just before you cross a gravel road. Follow the white blaze of the Appalachian Trail back into the woods. When we went through here there was a plaid blanket hanging over a tree branch. Did a through hiker meet a skunk and abandon his blanket? Or lose it? Was it too hot and just an extra weight?

Dark green Christmas fern grows here, along with several kinds of mushrooms. It's easy walking and there's time to enjoy the woods around you. You cross a small brook, and then twenty minutes farther along descend to a wide brook that you cross on stepping stones. Up a small rise, an overgrown woods road crosses the trail. Soon you

The views from the south peak are special.

descend a long flight of stone stairs to Brackett Brook, which you cross on a log bridge. The trail crews have done a great job here, both to increase your comfort and to protect the area from erosion.

Polypody ferns decorate a large rock as you start uphill again, through wood sorrel on the ground and past a deformed tree that looks like it would be a good place to sit—if you had six feet of snow under you so you could reach the inviting seat.

The climb becomes steeper as you travel uphill through a forest of large beeches. At a switchback to the south and up another long hill, a view down through the trees to Upper Baker Pond makes you realize that you're getting up higher. After about one and one-half hours out, you come to a small pile of rocks on the right-hand side of the trail; a perfect child-sized rock armchair here fits adults too, if you need a respite. Watch out, though—it might be a troll king's woodland throne.

There are more rock steps, and blue berries on clintonia plants just before another switchback. A worried-sounding red squirrel squeals at you, and then the trail makes several short switchbacks, and winds through birch woods into mixed woods again. Go uphill, past and over ledges in which some of the underlying quartz on this area begins to appear. Quite suddenly you are at a junction with signs for the north and south peaks. A five-minute walk takes you up over some great ledges to the south peak, where you look out at Smart's Mountain, the next height south on the Appalachian Trail.

Stay only a little while so that you'll have time to enjoy the north peak. It's about a fifteen-minute walk across a ridge to some spectacular soft green quartzite ledges, tinged with copper and smoothly polished by ancient glaciers and thousands of years of weather. In June the pink flowers of abundant sheep laurel soften the lines of the ledge. In September sheep laurel's grey-green leaves are beautiful, too. The views from here are splendid.

The trip down will give you more time to enjoy the silvery beech woods, the seasonal flowers and birds, and the birch forest with its mastlike, tall and sturdy trees.

15. Holt's Ledge

Walking distance: 2.2 miles
Walking time: 2 hours
Lyme, New Hampshire

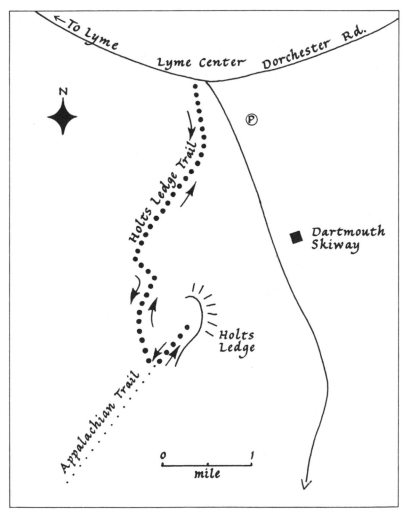

EONS AGO OUR CONTINENT AND AN AFRICAN continent collided, and mountains were pushed up along the collision zone. Much later, the land mass split and the two pieces drifted farther and farther apart, eventually forming the Atlantic Ocean. During this time a series of volcanoes developed in New England, most of them in what is now western New Hampshire. The bases of these volcanoes, eroded by glaciers and other erosive forces, contain many of the granites of the White Mountains. The rocks exposed between Hanover and Glencliff are mostly volcanic, moved upwards, and supported by what is called quartzite upturned shelf rock. Try to picture a mile-deep glacier moving slowly down the continent, carving the valleys, leaving the cliffs, rivers, and ponds we see today. Holt's Ledge is part of this history, as well as the story of the social development of the Connecticut River Valley.

The walk to Holt's Ledge leads you through a woods, and past old stone walls that indicate former pasture land, as do the young hardwoods you pass through. The trail is fairly easy and affords a look at many varieties of ferns and wildflowers. You're likely to hear warblers and thrushes singing, perhaps the drum of a woodpecker on a dead tree trunk. The trail is especially lovely beneath pastel-colored spring leaves, and in the splash of autumn colors.

There's always a reward at the top of a climb, even if it's only lunch or time to catch your breath. This trail's open summit looks out over ancient ledges, a pleasant valley, and ponds and mountains in the distance. You might spot peregrine falcons nesting in mountain ledges. You can picnic in a midsummer breeze, and perhaps chat with a through hiker on his or her last leg of the long trek from Georgia to Maine, for Holt's Ledge is on the Appalachian Trail.

ACCESS

Travel NH 10 north from Hanover, and in the village of Lyme bear right onto the road to Lyme Center, which is 1.7 miles farther on. Go through Lyme Center and continue for 1.5 miles to reach a fork in the road, from which you can see the chairlifts of the Dartmouth Skiway ahead. The left fork is the Lyme-Dorchester Road. On the right-hand side of the fork, on a tree, is an orange Dartmouth Outing Club trail sign and the white oblong blaze of the Appalachian Trail. This is your trailhead. You can park your car in a clearing just ahead on the left-hand side of the road, in front of the pond at the Skiway.

TRAIL

Your path is clearly blazed throughout, mostly on trees, by the white oblong paint patches of the Appalachian Trail and the orange-and-black stripes of the Dartmouth Outing Club.

Beyond the sign and just past a purple flowering raspberry bush, enter the woods up a steep short rise and then walk through maple and birch woods, past an old maple log ruffled in tiny fungi on a background of soft green moss. There's a seldom-running brook on your right. The floor of these woods is rich with woodsia and Christmas ferns, partridgeberry and wild oats. The trail levels out and you pass through a forest of gray birches, their leaves a pale green in the spring and sunshine yellow in the fall.

The walking is comfortable as the trail runs along a broken-down stone wall. The path bends right past a large birch. You cross through another stone wall and meet a service road for the ski area.

Look northward down the road. On a clear day you can glimpse part of Smarts Mountain, the next major height north of you on the Appalachian Trail. Cross the road to continue a gradual uphill walk in the woods. Cross another wall and in a few minutes you'll reach a junction with trail signs nailed to a tree. The signs tell you that you're only .5 mile from Holts Ledge and .6 from the road where you started.

Now you go up more steeply for about fifteen minutes, through a dense woods of slender young birch and beech trees, until you reach a former ski trail that looks more like a woods road. Two white oblong blazes on a tree tell you to turn right to continue. Ground pine bears candlelike cones beside horsetail plants, goldenrod, and black-eyed Susan; whorled asters bloom in mid- and late summer. A very old birch bears a line of oblong holes where the pileated woodpecker has been at work. If you're lucky, this great redcapped denizen of the woods might spread his broad wings and soar overhead.

The ski trail widens and goes uphill to the left. On the curve, watch for the trail sign that leads you to the right, back into the woods. Climb another steep hill for about ten minutes more. You'll see the sky ahead of you, and as you reach the top, the ledges that stick out over the valley across the fence. Unfortunately, erosion problems have necessitated a fence between you and the ledge where one used to be able to sit. But turn left and walk along the fence, and a field will open before you with rocks to sit upon and views that make you forget about the fence.

You'll see the sky ahead of you as you near the top.

Directly across the small valley is Winslow Ledge. The mountain to your left with the fire tower on top is Smarts Mountain. West of it is Mount Cube. Straight ahead you see Mount Cardigan's granite summit; beyond Mount Cardigan, almost to the horizon and to the right, is the jagged profile of Ragged Mountain. Mount Kearsarge stands in the distance to the southeast, and Mount Ascutney nearly due south, in Vermont. The large pond that shimmers below you is Goose Pond; the smaller one is Clark Pond.

There are strawberries on the slope in June, and an incredible field of orange and yellow columbine down the hill toward the ski lift. black-eyed Susan and goldenrod dance in the field in midsummer breezes, and an orange butterfly flutters its wings over the goldenrod on a hot August day.

Return the way you came. The trip down takes an hour to enjoy, or forty minutes if you're in a hurry.

16. Moose Mountain

Walking distance: 4 miles
Walking time: 3½ hours
Etna, New Hampshire

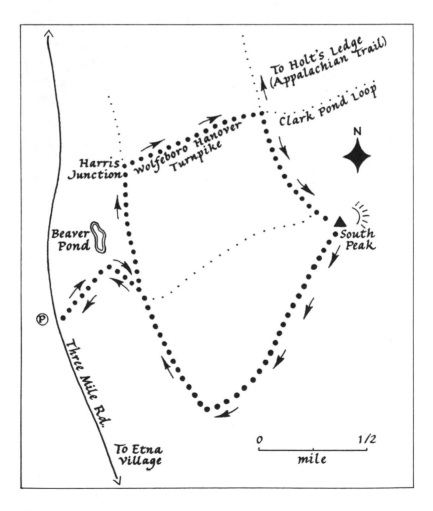

To Holt's Ledge
(Appalachian Trail)

Clark Pond Loop

N

Harris Junction

Wolfeboro Hanover Turnpike

Beaver Pond

South Peak

℗

Three Mile Rd.

To Etna Village

0   1/2

mile

MOOSE MOUNTAIN IS A LONG, LOW RIDGE WHICH
runs north to south, from just below Lyme to just above Mascoma
Lake, in New Hampshire. Its south peak, on the Appalachian Trail,
makes an enjoyable destination, especially since there are three trails
to the summit and you can take a loop walk by choosing two of them,
one up and the other down. The one we've chosen to take you up
on was, in 1772, the Wolfeboro to Hanover Turnpike. There are in-
frequent signs on trees to denote this fact. You may wonder how
stagecoaches made their way over the rutted road it must have been,
and still is.

Of the three trails mentioned, two are better blazed than the third,
and we recommend that you use these two. The third one goes between
the other two and is overgrown in places, not as well maintained as
the others, and marked by extremely faded blazes. This trail can be
followed, but not easily.

ACCESS

Leave Exit 18 from I-89 and drive north on NH 120 for 3.5 miles.
From Hanover, travel south on NH 120 until you're .7 mile from the
Food Co-op. Turn right (or left, coming from Hanover) at the traffic
lights, onto the road to Etna Village. Go 2 miles to a fork and signs.
Turn left and drive 1.4 miles to Rudsboro Road. Turn right and
continue for 1.6 miles past two more forks to arrive at Three Mile
Road, on the left. Follow this road 1.5 miles. After 1.3 miles, at the
top of a long hill, you'll see Appalachian Trail signs to Moose Mountain. This is *not* your trailhead. Continue down to the bottom of the
hill. On your left is a wide parking place. On your right is an arrow
trail-sign on a tree: begin your walk here.

TRAIL

Your trail is very well marked by blue blazes of paint on trees. Follow
the path through a pine woods, over a stone wall, and sharply downhill
to two plank bridges across a brook. Upstream to your left is a beaver
pond that you can cut through the woods to visit. Dead trees stand
tall in the pond, providing perches for red-winged blackbirds in the
spring.

Return to the bridges and follow the trail across them and up into
the woods. After about ten minutes you will meet an old road. Turn
left onto this road and walk about .5 mile to the Harris Trail Junction,

where there are signs for the Harris Trail and the Clark Pond Loop.

Turn right or east-southeast up the Harris Trail toward the Clark Pond Loop. Did you bring your flower guidebook for this flower-lovers' delight? In the early spring you'll see the tall downy violet, the foam flower, baneberry, adder's tongue, spring beauty, and many others. Your path climbs gradually uphill, and though it has a couple of steeper places, there are enough nearly flat interruptions to keep it from becoming strenuous.

You'll soon reach a junction of the Appalachian Trail and the Harris Trail, with signs on your left. Turn right (south). This narrow, winding trail is blazed with the white oblongs of the Appalachian Trail. It runs very gradually uphill in open woods. You'll see starflowers, clintonia, Canada mayflower, and wood sorrel (its shamrocklike leaf has a lemony taste and is refreshing to chew on a hot day—Indians used it for a lemonade-type drink). You might also see deer tracks, but as always, the deer themselves are elusive and chances of seeing one are few. You'll pass an open grassy spot and a bog; shortly thereafter the trail winds to your left and comes out in a clearing that is the south peak of Moose Mountain.

There are fine views from here, and it's a good lunch spot. Goose Pond (the nearer one) and Clark Pond lie below you, with Mount Cardigan to the east and Mount Kearsarge and then Ragged Mountain to the southeast. When there are not too many leaves on the trees, you can see Smarts Mountain and Mount Moosilauke to the north. The area at the summit of the south peak was cleared in November of 1968 when a passenger plane crashed and a helicopter landing field was needed for rescue operations.

To continue your walk, find the trail opening at the southern end of the clearing, and once again, the white oblong blazes of the Appalachian Trail. The trail drops around to the right and then into a long downhill stretch through a forest of white birches. The forest becomes a mixture of maples, beeches, poplars, and more birches. Princes pine and club mosses hug the ground.

Before you know it you reach the old road again. To return to where you started, turn right onto the old road and walk a very few minutes to cross a wide brook (unless the runoff has dried up), then up a slight rise until you see a blue-blazed tree on a path to your left. Follow the blue blazes back the way you came, across the two log bridges, up the hill, and out of the woods to your car.

This is a nice hike at any time of the year. It's fun on snowshoes.

Fungus decorates a tree on the path to the summit of Moose Mountain.

17. Gile Mountain

Walking distance: 1½ miles
Walking time: 1 hour
Norwich, Vermont

THE WALK TO THE FIRE TOWER ON TOP OF GILE
Mountain makes a great young-family hike. Small children will enjoy
the several varieties of flowers and mushrooms along the trail, and
perhaps also a downy woodpecker hammering an ancient tree trunk
in search of lunch. It's a short trip. The summit fire tower rewards
you with great views of the Upper Connecticut River Valley.

ACCESS

Follow Norwich's main road straight through the center of town. In

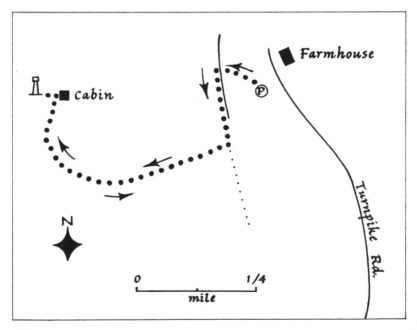

about .7 mile, just before a long hill, turn left onto Turnpike Road. Follow this road for about 6 miles. It turns to dirt, narrows, and climbs along a sheltered valley. Shortly after it levels out there's an old farmhouse on the right, and an open area on the left where signs invite you to park for the Tower Trail.

TRAIL

A small sign on a tree steers you onto the trail. Follow the arrow onto a logging road that you amble along through an open hardwood forest. Kick autumn leaves as you go. Climb over a couple of fallen trees and follow a narrower trail that bends right, away from the logging road. A sign tells you that this property is protected by the Nature Conservancy. You soon cross a log bridge and start uphill. Traverse a wide swath beneath some power lines and look eastward to New Hampshire hills across the Connecticut River. A large stand of old birches marks the way back into the woods. Easy switchbacks lead you through blackberry bushes, then over a gentle ridge, past a cabin on your right. Turn left at the cabin to visit the tower. Return the way you came.

Cross a log bridge.

18. Happy Hill

Walking distance: 6 miles
Walking time: 4 hours
Norwich, Vermont

THE PICTURESQUE VILLAGE OF NORWICH, VER-
mont was one of the earliest settlements on the upper Connecticut
River. The town was organized and its officers were named at a meeting in Mansfield, Connecticut in 1761. Like many of the river towns,
it was peopled by Connecticut pioneers who had given up on poor
soil and sought more fertile land to farm. In 1761 the six square miles
which would become Norwich were covered with primitive forest
unchanged by man. Bands of Indians traveled through occasionally,
and once in a while white hunters passed through from other parts
of New England. The French and Indian Wars were nearly over, and
immigrants from Canada and citizens of New England towns began
to settle the wilderness. When they came they cleared the land for
farms, saving the best of the 400-year-old pine trees for masts for His
Majesty's Navy. Dense forests made the lowlands too wet for farming,
so most farms were established on high land above the river.

Norwich became more desirable to settlers when, in 1769, Dartmouth College was founded in Hanover, just a ferry ride across the
river. The college promised educational as well as vocational opportunities for local citizens. The first bridge to Hanover was built in
1794. Norwich University, founded in Norwich in 1819, was originally
called the American Literary, Scientific, and Military Academy. It
was a unique school in New England because it was nonsectarian.
Politics and religion were excluded from its curriculum in the belief
that without them students would become unbigoted, patriotic, useful
citizens with attitudes suited to the character of a free people. Norwich
University, now located in Northfield Vermont, remains a thriving
institution today.

Our walk is on Happy Hill, just outside of Norwich, where some
of the early farms were. Though the stone walls are still evident, most
of the farms are gone and forest grows in their fields. The walk is

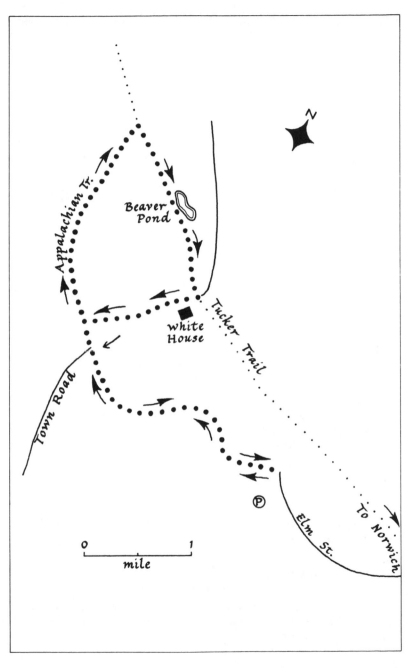

Beaver Pond

Appalachian Tr.

White House

Tucker Trail

Town Road

Elm St.

To Norwich

℗

N

0   1
mile

aptly named. It's a gentle trail offering much diversity—hardwoods and pine forest, farm fields, forest paths, and town roads. Part of it is on the Appalachian Trail. Easy walking gives you the chance to enjoy the beauty around you.

ACCESS

Reach the village of Norwich from I-91, US 5, or on local roads from Hanover, New Hampshire. There's a bandstand in the center of the village, opposite Elm Street. Turn onto Elm Street and travel approximately .8 mile to a wide shoulder on your left, where you can park your car. A few steps uphill and you'll see the white oblong blaze of the Appalachian Trail, also on your left. This is your trailhead.

TRAIL

Enter the woods between a felled tree and its large stump, and immediately go down into a dingle with fern-covered banks. In five minutes you'll walk uphill into mixed woods. Watch for the double, white, oblong blaze on a tree indicating a change in direction. The trail goes to the right here and then steadily uphill to a ledgy ridge where, if you're lucky, you might spot a deer.

In the fall of the year the forest floor is an outdoor Oriental rug. Red and orange maple leaves and yellow birch and beech leaves create an intricate pattern to walk upon.

Half an hour from the start there's light up ahead, and then you come into a clearing for power lines. The ferns are rust colored in October, accented by the white blooms of pearly everlasting. On clear days there's a view south to Wilder Dam on the Connecticut River. Re-enter the woods to the west across the clearing and travel over an almost level ridge. Pass a couple of dead trees full of woodpecker holes, and a grove of older hemlocks that make for a cool forest on hotter days. Go down into another dingle to a double blaze that directs you sharply to your right and then uphill, where the trail levels out again.

The woods keep changing and are a pleasure to walk through. Half an hour after you leave the power lines you cross a four-way junction. Be sure to stay with the white blazes—some old, washed-out pink ones might confuse you. Descend a small hill and turn right. Nuthatches peep at you now, and chickadees call their *dee, dee, dee.* Blue

Go down into a dingle with fern covered banks.

jays screech. The trail bears right over some ledges, through more ferns, and onto yet another ridge. Every now and then quartz rocks appear, common to the ancient geology of the river valley. Walk through the white pine forest and cross a stone wall that some farmer laboriously built a long time ago. The pine-cushioned path is soft underfoot.

Soon you cross a town road that you'll later return to. Once across the road, walk westward again into the woods. Notice the little cedar ground pine. The woods are sunlit as you leave the pines to walk across the hill and downhill through hardwoods again. There are some very large maples; the forest is white with birches. At another stone wall apples lie on the ground beneath a gnarled old tree, its branches grown high overhead trying to reach the sun. It's so quiet in these woods that you can't believe you hear traffic, probably from I-91 in the distance. The birches grow all the way down the hillside beside you. From where you are some low hills appear through the trees. Go down the hill, switchback up past a stand of birches by a wall, a tree trunk covered with several kinds of fungus, and an ancient maple tree.

About two and one-half hours into the walk you meet an old farm road. Turn right onto it—it's the Dartmouth Outing Club's Tucker Trail, a wide road edged with raspberries and blackberries. You pass a couple of ponds full of cattails. Asters, ferns, and stone walls border the road. Blue chicory blooms all summer. The road becomes wider and seems more traveled now. You pass a schoolhouse on your right.

When you reach two mailboxes and a newspaper box on your left, with a road and a white farmhouse uphill on your right, leave the Tucker Trail and turn right (the Tucker Trail continues downhill into Norwich). Walk along the road past open farm fields. Enjoy views eastward to Moose Mountain in New Hampshire, and wide meadows where dark green pinewoods stand in relief against brighter-hued maples. The driveable part of this road ends at a red farmhouse with a large old barn on the right-hand side of the road. There's a sign that says "Class 4 Road, Not Maintained." Walk straight ahead, past the sign.

Once you're just beyond the open fields, up a hill and back into woods, watch carefully for the white Appalachian Trail blazes on trees to either side of the road. There are usually orange ribbons tied around the trees beneath the blazes. This is where you crossed the road earlier. Take the trail on your left, and walk east to retrace your walk, back through the woods for about 1¼ miles to your car.

19. Pine Park

Walking distance: 2 miles
Walking time: 1½ hours
Hanover, New Hampshire

IN 1905 A GROUP OF HANOVER CITIZENS SET ASIDE
this old growth pine forest to preserve for ecological studies. Excepting
its groomed path for quiet walks, jogging, and cross-country skiing
along the Connecticut River, the woods remain undisturbed. You'll
hear and see birds, count innumerable varieties of flowers, find mushrooms and lichens and a unique display of many kinds of ferns.
Whether you live in the Hanover area or are just visiting, you'll find
Pine Park a most worthwhile distraction. You really should bring a
flower (or bird or fern or mushroom) guidebook with you for there
are so many to identify.

ACCESS

From the center of Hanover face the Baker Library clock tower, north,
and turn right along East Wheelock Street, then immediately left onto
College Street. Travel three blocks, or .4 mile, to Maynard Street.
Turn left and go past the hospital to the next street, which is Rope
Ferry Road. Turn right. In half a mile you will reach the end of the
road and the golf course. Your walk commences straight ahead, on a
road marked by a sign that you should read. It tells you where you
are, your responsibilities, and those of the proprietors.

TRAIL

Walk down the road along the golf course until you see a long bridge
overhead. Bear left, downhill into a deep ravine, to meet a crossroad.
Turn left onto this road and stroll beside Girl Brook beneath tall
hemlocks and even taller pines. On the ground are lush ferns—regal
ostrich fern waving in gentle breezes, sensitive fern, oak fern, rare
maidenhair, and bracken (you may see some that we missed). In some
places the ferns cover the banks of the steep hillsides. Pale blue Low-

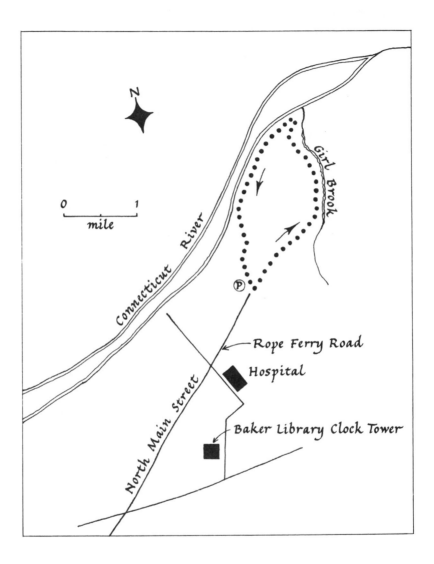

rie's asters and snow-white snakeroot bloom most of the summer along much of this path. American yew covers the bank on the left; in August the "doll's eyes" of the baneberry hang from its stem. The forest soon becomes populated with more birch and maple than evergreen, and at just under .5 mile you cross the brook and go slightly uphill to leave this splendor behind you. But there's more to come.

Hear and see birds, count innumerable varieties of flowers, find mushrooms and lichens. . . .

Once beyond the brook, follow the trail to the left. Within a minute you will get a glimpse of the Connecticut River. There's a tiny side path on your right. Detour here for a ten-minute round trip and fine sights of the river. There are good lunch spots along its banks in case you brought yours and would like to sit a spell. Birds may sing you a concert, and perhaps a canoe will slip silently by.

Back on the main trail, hundred-foot pines tower over the hemlocks, and the wide path feels soft underfoot with pine needles. In the adjacent woods Indian pipe and several varieties of mushroom poke up through the russet-colored forest floor. The river flows southward beside you now for nearly a mile, and you'll see several more side paths leading down to its shore. There are more flowers where the trees are not so dense, including clintonia with its yellow bells in the spring and its bright blue berries in the fall, and Canada mayflower.

The trail leaves the river to climb uphill past banks covered with young hemlocks. The golf course is at the top of the rise. Continue on the road past the number 3 tee. Now turn left onto the paved road and walk up the hill between the Dartmouth Outing Club House and the Golf Club, to Rope Ferry Road, where you started.

20. Velvet Rocks

Walking distance: 4 miles
Walking time: 3 hours
Hanover, New Hampshire

THE WALK ALONG THE APPALACHIAN TRAIL TO
Velvet Rocks takes you through a lovely woods embellished by flowers in the spring, brightly colored leaves in the fall, and lots of handsome granite ledges. When you arrive at the polypody fern–covered rocks, relax upon a deep mat of soft pine needles and enjoy the pine woods and the views of hills to the east.

ACCESS

At the northeast corner of Chase Field, behind the Dartmouth Co-op Food Store and the radio antenna, there's a sign at the trailhead and the white oblong blaze of paint on a tree that indicates the Appalachian Trail. This is the beginning of your trip.

TRAIL

Cross a small bridge at the white blaze and go immediately left, to walk parallel to the athletic field into a hemlock woods, and then up some rock steps. A couple of open spaces along here give you views of Baker Tower and the college campus. Trailing arbutus blooms in the spring, and partridgeberries glow red in the fall. Gray-green reindeer lichen accents the moss-covered rocks.

The trail leads uphill, bends to the left, and runs under some high ledges. Stone steps lead to a switchback and then across a gentle ridge. You reach a junction with signs that direct you to turn left for the Velvet Rocks Shelter. You should bear right to continue on the Appalachian Trail, along another ridge and down through fern-covered rocks and a beech forest to another junction with more signs.

Your trail goes right, steeply uphill, back into a hemlock forest, and then steeply downhill into a dingle. Cross the dingle and climb

80

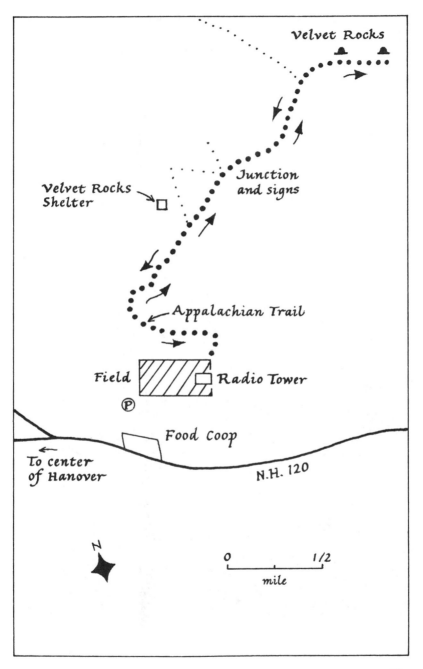

Velvet Rocks

Velvet Rocks
Shelter

Junction
and signs

Appalachian Trail

Field   Radio Tower

Food Coop

To center
of Hanover

N.H. 120

N

0   1/2
mile

steeply uphill, again through graceful hemlocks and eventually to a sign to Trescott Road.

Turn right to follow the white blazes into a garden of pine trees and the aptly named Velvet Rocks.

Return the same way and enjoy your walk back as much as you enjoyed the trip in.

Up the stone steps.

21. Mount Tom

Walking distance: 3 miles
Walking time: 1½ hours
Woodstock, Vermont

LEADING OUT OF THE EXQUISITE VILLAGE OF
Woodstock there is a network of walking trails through lovely woods
to easily accessible summits, where you can feast your eyes on views
of river, farmland, rolling hills, and Vermont mountains, as well as
the picturesque village below you. This walk will take you on a loop
that connects two very pleasant trails.

ACCESS

Woodstock is easily reached via signed exits from I-91 and I-89, and
US 4. There is public parking in the village, and the trailheads are
within easy walking distance from the village green, opposite the
famous Woodstock Inn.

TRAIL

From the green, walk west on Mountain Avenue, through the covered
bridge to River Street. Turn right onto River Street. At the north
edge of the cemetery turn left onto the Bridle Trail. Signs will tell
you that you are on a combination bridle and hiking trail.

Stroll along the trail for about .2 mile to reach the Girl Scout cabin
on your left. Immediately past the cabin are yellow blazes and a woods
trail, also on your left. Go into the woods and follow this trail through
open forest, across a small brook to trail signs. You want the Precipice
Trail, which leads to the right. Follow directional arrows and yellow
blazes on the trees. There are quite splendid displays of many varieties
of ferns through here. You'll reach a bench and another Precipice
Trail sign directing you to turn right, beneath a high cliff.

Soon you begin a steady and steep uphill climb. A couple of open
ledges give you the town and farm fields to look at. The church clock
in the valley strikes the hour. The trail bends left at three yellow

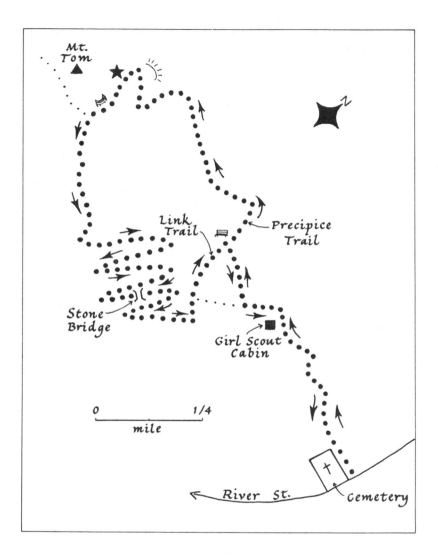

Mt. Tom

Link Trail

Precipice Trail

Stone Bridge

Girl Scout Cabin

0   1/4
mile

River St.

Cemetery

blazes, then right, and winds around the ledges. Pass a North Peak Trail sign on your right. Your trail continues southwest. As it gets steeper and more precipitous, chains strung beside the path keep both you and the soil from sliding downhill. You'll climb switchbacks and pass between great rocks, dumped off, no doubt, by melting glaciers ten thousand years ago. Now they're blanketed in polypody ferns. The pileated woodpecker has left his holes in a dead tree. Follow the

84

chains until you come out on a wide-open ledge. Turn left here to pass the Woodstock Christmas star on a tower to your right. You have reached the south peak of Mount Tom when you come to a hitching post for horses and a circular bench for you to sit upon and observe the view.

Killington Peak, to the west, rises high above the King Farm in the foreground. To the left is US 4. To the south, Mount Ascutney dominates the horizon. Below and to the east is the north end of Kedron Valley, and then the Woodstock Inn. Left of the Inn is the County Courthouse and the covered bridge. The bare knob of Mount Peg rises above the bridge (see Walk 22 in this book). Eastward from there is the Congregational Church, to the north of the river is the Billings Farm, and then the mountains of New Hampshire.

Once you've enjoyed all this for a while, walk on the road sixteen steps past the bench. Just below the road a sign on a tree says "Mountain Avenue." Begin your walk down from this sign. The trail drops steeply at first, then follows gentle switchbacks all the way. You'll see little paths where shortcuts have been taken—please follow the trail as indicated by the more apparent path. Erosion is a problem here, and the trails have been built with the protection of these fine woods in mind.

When you're nearly down you cross a stone bridge and reach a sign that says "Faulkner Trail," and then one that says "Link Trail." Follow the Link Trail back to the Precipice Trail and the bench you passed on your way up. Turn right to retrace your steps to the cemetery and into the village.

22. Mount Peg

Walking distance: 1½ miles
Walking time: 1¼ hours
Woodstock, Vermont

WHETHER YOU'RE FORTUNATE ENOUGH TO BE staying in Woodstock or are just passing through, this walk provides a nice travel respite, bringing you quickly to wonderful views of mountains, rolling hills, and the farmlands that make Vermont the special place that it is.

ACCESS

From the village green in Woodstock, walk or drive southeast on Court Street to Cross Street. Turn left and then almost immediately right onto Golf Avenue. On your left, opposite Maple Street, is a place to park. Just up a paved driveway there's a sign on a tree that directs you to Mount Peg.

TRAIL

Yellow rectangular blazes on the trees mark this entire trail, though sometimes you have to look for them. A number of unmarked trails branch off from the main trail, so be sure to watch for the blazes. There are several easy switchbacks on your trail through some very tall pines, whose fallen needles make a soft path to walk upon. After a short, steep climb starts you on the trail, turn right and then very soon left, uphill, to a low bench beneath a gnarled beech tree. Turn left and go uphill to another low bench at the top of the rise, and then turn right toward a yellow blaze. You soon cross a clearing with some especially nice white pines growing in it. At the edge of the clearing your path leads to the right again.

Pass beneath the power lines and cross an avenue of spruce trees. Turn left at an old stone wall into an orchard of old-fashioned thornapple trees. Just past the orchard you will come into open fields and face two open slopes. A tree at the bottom of these slopes has two

86

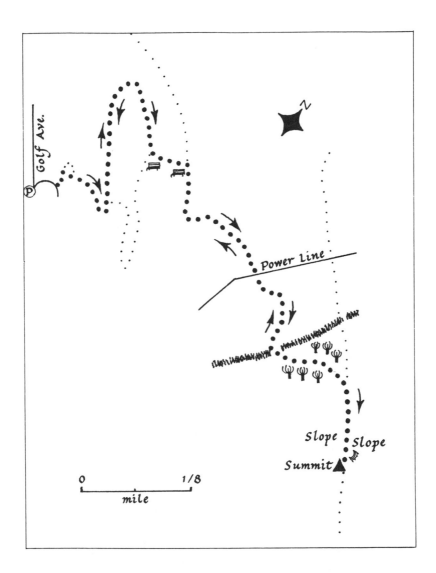

Golf Ave.

Power Line

Slope

Slope

Summit

0   1/8

mile

yellow blazes on it. Take the left slope and follow the yellow blazes to the top of the hill, where there is a great circular bench. You are at the summit of Mount Peg.

From here you have a 180-degree view. Across from you is Mount Tom with its precipitous ledges; beyond it are the hills of Pomfret. Killington Mountain rises way to the left, and away to the right Mount

Ascutney's profile defines the horizon. The Billings Farm lies below you in the foreground just beyond a bend in the Ottauquechee River.

On your descent be sure to watch for the blazes that take you back through the orchard. They are directly at the bottom of the hill, but it's quite easy to go past them in the wrong direction. Remember to go through the orchard, and watch for the turn when you come to the low green bench. The road continues, but you must be sure to go left, down the hill, and then right at the second bench, to retrace your steps.

The pine needle covered trail is soft to walk upon.

23. Carl's Walk

Walking distance: 7½ miles
Walking time: 6 hours
Between Woodstock and Barnard, Vermont

A DAY TRIP ALONG THE APPALACHIAN TRAIL RE-
wards you with 270-degree views from Luce's Lookout. Edwin Luce,
a descendant of one of the original settlers of the town of Barnard,
built a tower at the Lookout in 1894, "for the pleasure of himself and
all other lovers of nature." He lashed three spruce trees with wire and
erected a rough platform on top of them. At the base of the ladder
that led to the platform was a pay-as-you-go sign, requesting a dime
from each visitor to help maintain the tower.

Luce's Lookout was something of a local sensation. An area of about
three-fourths of an acre was set out for picnic tables, benches, and
two outhouses, as well as a pole fence for tying horses to. As many
as fifty visitors came to enjoy the views on nice Sunday afternoons.

Luce replaced his makeshift tower with a tall wooden structure that
had an anterior stairway and a sheltered platform at the top. This
structure collapsed years later due to the neglect of subsequent owners
of the property. Now there's a private camp up there with a rather
steep ladder, well worth climbing to the "widow's watch" on the roof.
On clear days you can see east to the Presidential Range in New
Hampshire, north to Camel's Hump and Mount Mansfield in Vermont, and south to Killington Mountain's ski slopes and Shrewsbury
Peak. You can look down through the trees to Lakota Lake. In 1891
a group of fishermen was issued a charter for a private club there that
is still in operation. In the days before cars the anglers and their
families journeyed from Woodstock to Lakota by horse and buggy.
If they stayed for dinner at the club, someone usually had to walk in
front of the horse with a lantern in order to find the way home down
the wooded road.

One local legend about the Lookout tells of Mr. Luce's plan for a
signal system to announce the election of William McKinley to the
Presidency by means of a fire on Mount Kearsarge in New Hampshire,

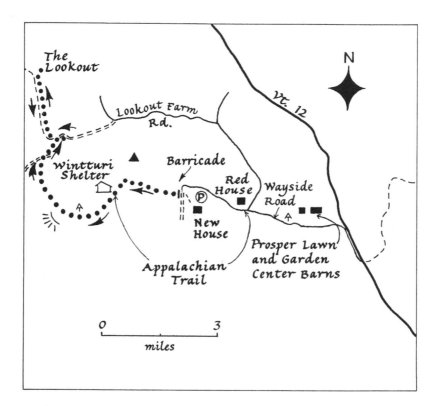

one on Luce's Lookout, and finally one on Mount Mansfield in northern Vermont. We couldn't find any record of whether this ever did take place.

While the Lookout is private property, the owners welcome walkers who will enjoy the view while treating their property with respect.

ACCESS

Follow VT 12 north out of Woodstock from its junction with US 4. You will pass a historic marker that commemorates the first skiers' rope tow in the United States. Stay on VT 12. You'll soon see a black-and-white sign directing you to turn left for the Prosper Lawn and Garden Center. At 4.4 miles from Woodstock, turn left onto Wayside Road and pass the barns on your right. Follow Wayside Road to its end, where there's a farm with a new house on the left and a barricaded road on your right. Just inside the barricade is an Appalachian Trail sign. Do not park here. Instead, turn around and go back, down the road on which you came, to the curve, where you'll see a wide shoulder on your right. Park here and walk back to the trailhead, uphill past a brook and a white birch forest and the farm.

TRAIL

Walk past the barricade onto an old road, past Christmas trees. Goldenrod fills the road in late summer. A rounded, spruce-covered hill stands by itself off to your right. The trail curves left past the round hill, and past blue-and-white blazes on a tree directly in front of you.

Luce's Lookout as it appeared around the turn of the century.

Standing club moss looks even more green than usual above the first snow of the season.

The trail leads southwest, and about half an hour after starting you reach the Appalachian Trail's Wintturi Shelter, named for a dedicated trail worker of the Green Mountain Club. The Appalachian Trail from VT 12 to Sherburne Pass is maintained by the Ottaquechee Section of the Green Mountain Club. From the shelter bear left where the sign says Appalachian Trail South, and follow a narrow trail through the woods. Go steadily uphill through logged slash, gradually at first and then more steeply, onto a ridge. You can see south through a notch. The trail curves west into a small dingle, then south up ledges into a spruce forest. A thick covering of deep green princes pine and club moss beautifies the floor of this forest. You may hear the whir of a grouse's wings, or catch a glimpse of one as it disappears into the trees.

Cross another old road, running north and south and marked by orange and blue bands around a tree. Go uphill across the road and continue on a gentle walk through birch woods to hill views that open up to the south. Now your path climbs uphill again, westward past double junction blazes. A long downhill section of trail leads you around a knob of granite ledges. The trail levels out beneath the hill, and after about half an hour along the level it meets an abandoned road. Turn right (north) and travel very briefly to another double blaze. Bear left to follow the white blazes until you meet a wide road. Turn left and walk along the road until you see an orange oblong blaze and a sign that directs you to turn right for the Lookout.

It's about a twenty-minute walk from here to the Lookout, through a forest rich with paper and yellow birches. The trail, another abandoned road, levels out. When the leaves have dropped from the trees, you can see the ski trails on Killington Mountain to the southwest. In early fall a great V-formation of geese flies overhead, honking as they go as if to say good-bye for the winter. The trail rises steeply again, and soon there's a junction where signs indicate that you're 2.9 miles from Wintturi Shelter and 400 feet from the Lookout. Go up a short, steep road to the cabin and take advantage of the ladder and the platform for spectacular views.

The hillsides below are bright with color in the fall. In the spring the softer colors of buds and new leaves are pleasing, too. In the summer you'll catch a breeze up here, and in the winter you'll see snow-capped mountains nearby and in the distance.

Sunapee, Dartmouth, and the Shadows of Mount Ascutney

24. Saint-Gaudens National Historic Site

Walking distance: ¾ mile
Walking time: 1 hour
Cornish, New Hampshire

THE HOME, STUDIOS, AND GARDENS OF AUGUSTUS Saint-Gaudens, one of America's greatest sculptors, are now a National Historic Site. A tour of the Park is indeed a contrast to walks through the woods and over the backroads described in this book. Here are manicured hedges of pine and hemlock, herringbone-patterned brick walks, formal gardens with pools fed by golden turtles. There is also a nice woodland walk into Blow Me Up Ravine.

Purchased originally as a summer residence, the house called Aspet was once a tavern along the stage road between Windsor, Vermont and Meriden, New Hampshire. The Saint-Gaudens remodeled the house and added the grand porch with its magnificent view of Mount Ascutney. During the artist's later years the family lived here year round, and the house and surrounding area became an artists' colony. Many painters, writers, actors, sculptors, and moneyed socialites of the late nineteenth century lived and worked in Cornish. For many years Aspet was the scene of parties and festivals where all the colony met. In June of 1905 friends and companions of Saint-Gaudens celebrated the twentieth anniversary of his coming to Cornish by staging a play based on a classical Greek drama. They erected a small Grecian temple, which was later reproduced in marble to become the family burial place.

After the death in 1907 of Augustus Saint-Gaudens, his widow and son provided for the preservation of this property. Later the New Hampshire legislature chartered the Saint-Gaudens Memorial as a nonprofit corporation to preserve and exhibit the artist's works. Friends and admirers of the sculptor have also supported the memorial's purpose. In 1964 Congress authorized the National Park Service to accept the property as a gift. A year later it was designated a

94

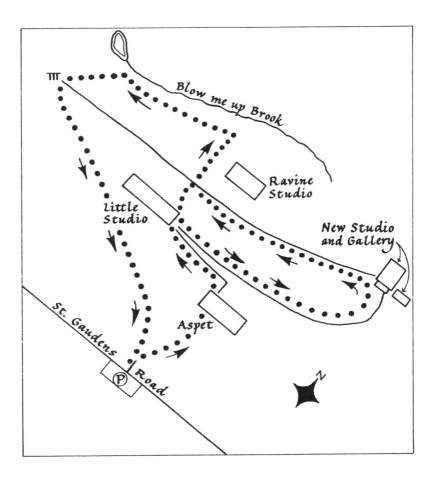

National Historic Site.

The site is open for tours, for a small fee, from May through October. Each summer the Saint-Gaudens Memorial sponsors concerts and exhibitions by contemporary artists. A visit here will not only take you back to the wonderful days of the colony at the turn of the century, but will entertain you with the arts of today.

Picnic tables are available in season for your comfort and pleasure.

ACCESS

Twelve miles north of Claremont and about 18 miles south of Hanover, on NH 12A, a sign for the park directs you to turn right or left, depending on the direction in which you are traveling. Drive up a long road through handsome woods to a parking area on your right. You can also come via I-91 and exit at Ascutney or Hartland, Vermont to NH 12A, or reach it from the West Lebanon exit of I-89.

Upon leaving your vehicle, cross the road to the path between the hedges and walk to the house, where a Park Service attendant will tell you how to visit the house, studios, and grounds.

TRAIL

After you visit Aspet and get a feeling for who this great man was and how he lived, walk outside through the formal gardens to the Little Studio to become acquainted with his work. This is where concerts are given on summer Sundays. When you leave the studio, by the rear door, turn right and amble through a lovely avenue of birch trees to the New Studio, where you can see more of the sculpture of Saint-Gaudens. You might be familiar with some of the work, even if you didn't know Saint-Gaudens' name before. You may have seen his Farragut Statue in Madison Square in New York, his Shaw Memorial on the Boston Common, or his Lincolns in Illinois.

Don't miss the picture gallery, which exhibits the works of modern artists during the visitor season.

Walk north from the gallery to the Ravine Studio. Sometimes you will see an artist at work here. Just past the studio, the Ravine Trail goes off to the right and down a steep hill to Blow Me Up Brook, named with tongue-in-cheek because of nearby Blow Me Down Brook. A nice trail hugs the bank beside the rippling brook. You'll see ferns and wildflowers beneath mixed species of trees. Ten minutes of walking brings you to a left-hand turn. A serene little pool lies beyond a picturesque cascade a few steps beyond the turn. Enjoy the view and then go back to the turn, uphill, to come out beside the Greek-style temple, where the Saint-Gaudens family is buried.

Turn left and stroll across the lawn toward Aspet, then on to the picnic tables and your car. If you'd like to walk longer, turn right at the temple and follow the walk described in this book as *Blow Me Down Natural Area.*

Manicured hedges, herringbone-patterned brick walks, formal gardens with pools fed by golden turtles.

25. Blow Me Down Natural Area

Walking distance: 1–2 miles
Walking time: 1–2 hours
Cornish, New Hampshire (Saint-Gaudens National Historic Site)

THE BLOW ME DOWN NATURAL AREA IS PART OF over eighty wooded acres protected by the National Park Service, and is adjacent to the Saint-Gaudens National Historic Site. Augustus Saint-Gaudens, one of our nation's most important sculptors, lived and worked here, finding inspiration for his life and work in the beautiful forests near his home.

The natural history of these woods predates the Ice Age, when the bedrock here formed as muddy sediment on the floor of an ancient sea. The erosion wrought by the glaciers helped to shape the hills, and created Mount Ascutney, which consists of erosion-resistant rock. Today you walk on sandy soil left by the glaciers, through woods that only a hundred years ago were cleared pastures and open meadows. Club mosses decorate the forest floor. Tall pine trees, once a mainstay of the local economy, grow on the steep slopes of the ravine. Trees such as these were cut for ships' masts for the Royal Navy, before the American Revolution. Hardwoods grow farther down, on the more level places. You shouldn't miss the sycamore trees, which are rare this far north. And enjoy the many varieties of flowers, ferns, and birds.

Cattails and yellow iris grow on the banks of the pond. Muskrat and heron live here. The beavers are always hard at work, and black ducks nest along the shore. The fall of water at the dam once powered a grist mill that, until 1928, served the needs of surrounding farms, grinding corn, oat, bran, and feeds for livestock.

These are peaceful woods to stroll through, offering much to learn if you remain aware of where you are and what you see. A guide to the area is available at the Saint-Gaudens studio; copies are also kept in a wooden box at the end of the trail, across the lawn from the Grecian temple. The pond is a nice place to picnic.

ACCESS

Saint-Gaudens National Historic Site is located just off NH 12A, 12 miles north of Claremont and 18 miles south of Hanover. If you travel I-89, take the West Lebanon, New Hampshire exit (Exit 20) and drive south on NH 12A. If you travel I-91, take Exit 8 and drive north, or take Exit 9 and drive south on NH 12A. There are signs as you approach Cornish, and a good sign at the entrance to the Saint-Gaudens Site. Your walk begins at the Site.

Drive up a long hill to the parking area on your right. Park and walk toward The Saint-Gaudens home (called Aspet). As you approach the home turn left and walk west toward the river, past the Grecian

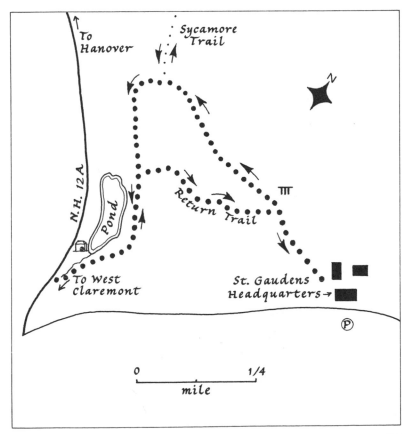

The grist mill once served the needs of surrounding farms, grinding corn, oats, bran and feed for livestock.

temple, until you see a trail sign and what is obviously a trail entering the woods.

TRAIL

Your way is well marked by small signs depicting a mill by a stream. The path runs downhill through tall pines, ferns, and mosses that are described in the guidebook. A sign at the bottom of the hill directs you to the Sycamore Trail, a worthwhile diversion. The trail leads to Blow Me Down Brook, where you will see the grove of sycamore trees on the opposite shore. A large, maple-like leaf, and scaly, peeling bark are the trademarks of the sycamore. There was once a wool mill here.

Go back to where you turned right for this trail, and follow the main trail as it bends to the left beneath the hill and then goes parallel to the road, along level ground to the pond. Notice the sign for the Return Trail, but for now pass it by on your way to the pond. If you brought your lunch, make use of the picnic table. Walk along the pond and enjoy its flowers, ferns, and perhaps some wood ducks. Eventually you will reach the old grist mill and the dam. Below the dam exquisite maidenhair fern hangs along the banks of the brook.

Once you've taken in all of this, go back to the Return Trail, which leads you up a small, steep hill, and then more gradually uphill through the ravine to the lawn opposite the temple. Amble over the lawn and enjoy the views of Aspet, and the massive hill to the west that is Mount Ascutney. We hope you'll have time to visit the house and studios of Augustus Saint-Gaudens (see walk 24).

26. The Pinnacle

Walking distance: 1 mile
Walking time: 1 hour
Wilgus State Park—Weathersfield, Vermont

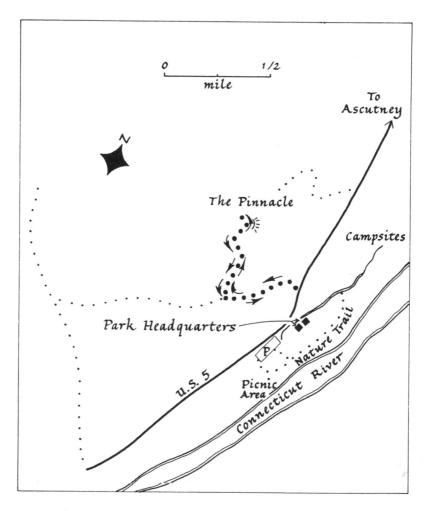

A WALK TO THE PINNACLE IN WILGUS STATE PARK

is a great leg stretcher if you're traveling through the Connecticut River Valley. Just below the summit are fine views of the river. The park is an ideal overnight stop for canoeists, bikers, and other campers with its picnic area and waterfront campsites. It's beautiful in foliage season—an exceptional little park.

ACCESS

Wilgus State Park is on US 5, 1.1 miles south of Ascutney, Vermont. It's 6 miles south of Windsor and 44 miles north of Brattleboro. In season there's a small fee to park there.

TRAIL

You'll see a trail sign directly across the street from park headquarters. The trail immediately rises steeply and then winds through open mixed woods. Frequent blue blazes on trees make it easy to follow. After the first steep climb you follow a woods road to a fork, bear right, and then left steeply uphill again and over some rock steps. Two blue blazes indicate a turn to the right. Hemlocks mix into the hardwoods. The trail winds right and then you're on an easy ridge high above the river. The hill falls away from you on the right. You get a glimpse of the river through birches, oaks, and pines, and suddenly you come to a wide opening in the trees where there's an excellent view of the river and New Hampshire hills across it. A breeze refreshes you. This is a fine spot to sit a spell and just enjoy.

Return the way you came. Or make a loop by following the blazes over the summit and down a winding path through the woods, back to US 5. You are about .3 mile from your car. Walk south, carefully, against traffic, along a very busy road.

27. Springweather Nature Area

Walking distance: about 2 miles
Walking time: 2½ hours
Weathersfield, Vermont

THE ASCUTNEY MOUNTAIN AUDUBON SOCIETY and the U.S. Army Corps of Engineers have developed the Springweather Nature Area for environmental studies by schools, organizations, and individuals. You are welcome to walk around it whether you've come to look, learn, or just relax. There are seventy acres of fields and forests, with several brooks and the Black River. Part of the trail overlooks a shallow lake that lies in the shadow of the rolling hills and Mount Ascutney.

Each season here shares something with you—migrating birds and flowers in the spring, a heron fishing in the pond below you in the summer, bright foliage, goldenrod, and apples and berries on abandoned farmland in the fall, great ski country in the winter. The marked trails are easy to follow, and strategically placed benches help you to rest and enjoy the views.

ACCESS

From the junction at Ascutney of US 5 and VT 131, follow VT 131 for 2.3 miles to a sign for Wellwood Orchards. Find Weathersfield Center Road on your left, and drive .3 mile through the historic village of Weathersfield Center to a right turn onto Wellwood Orchard Road. Follow it to the orchard store—a worthwhile stop. You can pick your own apples here and buy Vermont cheese. Continue along what becomes a gravel road that curves to the right and then come to a T junction. Turn left onto the paved road and then, almost immediately, turn right at the sign for Springweather Nature Area. Bear right at a fork and you'll see the parking area on your right.

104

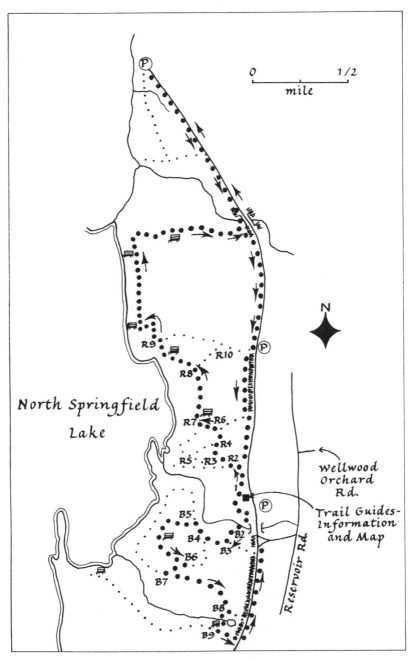

North Springfield
Lake

R9
R10
R8
R7 · R6
R4
R5 · R3 · R2

Wellwood
Orchard
Rd.

Trail Guides-
Information
and Map

B5
B4
B6
B7
B8
B9
B2
B3

Reservoir Rd.

N

0   1/2
    mile

105

TRAIL

Walk on the dirt road until you come to a map and bulletin board on your left. A brief study of the map will acquaint you with the site. The trees bear clear markers in red, blue, and green, indicating the three different trails.

Pass a bench and bear left with the blue arrow into some fine open woods. Your trail is edged with orange jewelweed and white poke-weed, in bloom in August. False Solomon's seal stems bend with the weight of autumn berries. The doll's eyes of the baneberry appear, and you'll see purple joe-pye weed and purple asters. In ten minutes you cross a brook, bear left past the Christmas fern, and climb uphill into a field of milkweed and goldenrod.

Turn right, past the bluebird house and back into more woods, and up a hill. Another blue arrow leads you straight ahead through a hemlock forest and to some wonderful viewpoints. You'll look across the lake to nearby hills, great Mount Ascutney with its transmittal towers on top, and what appears to be a planted pine forest. There's a bench down a little way for a brief rest. Return to the blue arrow on a birch tree.

The path runs between two birches and, becoming very narrow, bears right downhill into an open field. You'll reach a marker labeled B7.

Proceed left past the line of bluebird boxes and follow an indistinct trail along the right side of the field to the B8 marker. A narrow path on the right leads you across a stepping-stone dam of rocks. Arrow-heads bloom at the edge of the brook in summer. Pass a stand of raspberries and turn left, before the cornfield, onto the dirt road bordered with ferns, Queen Anne's lace, and old stone walls. Amble along the quiet road leading back to your car.

That was the blue trail. To extend your walk, go back to where you began and you'll see a red marker that points right where you turned left for the blue trail. Follow the red trail to a fork marked R2. Go right, uphill to another fork marked R6, where you bear left to come out on a grassy cliff above North Springfield Lake. Another small path leads to a bench. Down on the water, a duckling paddles into the cattails. A blue heron searches the shallow water for her lunch, while you eat yours. A fisherman launches his boat at the end of a dirt road, across the water.

Walk along the cliff and turn left on the trail, past blue chicory

Perhaps there's a fishing boat on the river below you.

flowers and another bench, onto a pine needle–covered path, to a junction with green markers. Woodpecker holes decorate dead trees. Deep gorges carry spring runoff down to the Black River. Circle the gorge to the left through a lush growth of ferns. Perhaps there's a fishing boat on the river below you. Turn right, away from the river, with the trail. Go downhill to meet the dirt road again. Turn left and follow the road to its end. You'll meet the river there, or turn right when you reach the road (at the end of the green trail), and complete your walk back to your car. These trails give you many options. They would also be nice to ski.

To help support all this you can join the Ascutney Mountain Audubon Society, join in their maintenance activities, or do both. To find out how, contact the Society at P.O. Box 191, Springfield, Vermont 05156. National Audubon members are automatically members of the Ascutney Mountain Audubon Society, but may wish to receive the newsletter.

28. The Bunker Place

Walking distance: 2 miles (add 1 mile to include Part 2)
Walking time: 2 hours (add 1 hour to include Part 2)
New London, New Hampshire

THE NEW LONDON CONSERVATION COMMISSION contains several trails to walk in areas where you can enjoy beauty, botany, and local history. The trip to the Bunker Place includes all three.

ACCESS

From the center of New London turn north onto Pleasant Street, which starts at the corner of Main Street beside the yellow Kidder Building. Travel 1.9 miles northeast to Pingree Road. Bear left and go .5 mile on Pingree Road, past a Cape Cod–style house high on your left, which, as the sign on it notes, was the home of Jeremiah Pingree, one of New London's earliest settlers. Just after you pass the Pingree house, the Hayes Woods barricade appears on your right. Park here at the edge of the road.

TRAIL

Part 1. A few feet past the barricade a trail sign on a tree points left. The trail enters the woods and goes through a carpet of myrtle. Some fallen-in shacks and foundation holes above a brook on the right could have been Nathaniel Bunker's sawmill—the town history of New London mentions that he had one on Great Brook. There is also, however, evidence of a sawmill farther on.

You'll soon come to a rickety bridge across a brook; stepping stones across another brook bring you to trail signs. Follow the signs to the Bunker Loop. Your way is well marked with frequent blazes. Bear left at a loop sign. Walk through a field of waist-high ferns, and, if you come in July, raspberries to sweeten your mouth. Pass a blaze on a beech tree and climb steadily upward for about thirty minutes. The forest is mostly spruce and hemlock now, its floor sheltered by hay-

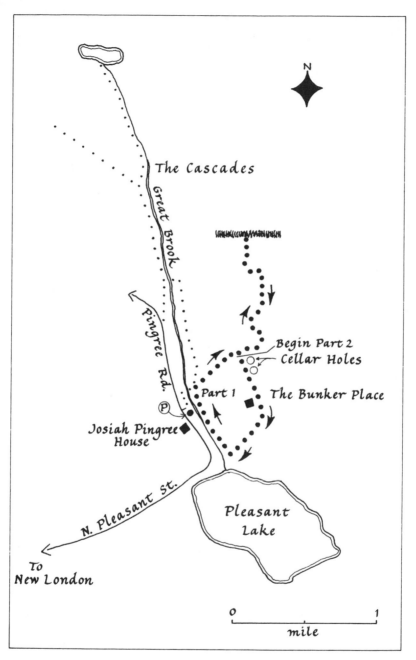

The Cascades

Great Brook

Pingree Rd.

Begin Part 2
Cellar Holes

Part 1

The Bunker Place

Ⓟ

Josiah Pingree
House

N. Pleasant St.

To
New London

Pleasant
Lake

N

0   mile   1

scented and bracken ferns. Although the climb is uphill it is not at all difficult. In the early spring you're liable to hear peepers from a snow-melt pond. Downy woodpeckers hammer, and white-breasted nuthatches run up and down tree trunks.

You're more than halfway when you go through a gap in a stone wall onto a thick blanket of haircap moss that you really should walk on barefoot, especially on a hot day after rain.

The woods open up here. Small gray birches grow beside your path, pale green reindeer lichen and brighter green ground pine beneath them. Soon you're walking on open ledges. Running club moss spirals next to juniper bushes laden with blue berries. Yellow St. Johnswort blossoms here in midsummer.

If you brought your lunch you'll be tempted to stop here, but wait a minute. The trail continues southeast. Straight ahead, past a pile of wood slabs which could also have been a sawmill, you'll reach two cellar holes in an open field, and some fine rocks to sit upon. Tall pines and dark green spruces border the field. Mount Kearsarge is your backdrop. This is definitely the lunch spot, unless you take Part 2 of this walk, which we highly recommend.

To complete Part 1 from the cellar holes, face the cellar holes and the mountain and turn right onto a wide road, south and downhill. Pass an enormous juniper at least 12 feet in diameter, and then a tremendous white birch growing out of a cellar hole. Stone walls edge what was probably the original Bunker farm. A lone pine stands across the street in a walled pasture. Two ancient apple trees still bear fruit in the southern corner of the field. Benjamin Bunker is reputed to have been a man of great muscular strength—he had to be to build these massive walls. It is also said that when he built his house he carried all the lumber for it on his back up this hill. What a fine place this must have been for Sunday visits and dooryard calls.

Before you continue down the road enjoy the vista of Mount Kearsarge across the fields, Pleasant Lake below you, and in the distance to the south, the long ridge of Mount Sunapee. A ten-minute stroll down the old farm road brings a gate to view with Pleasant Street beyond. Just before the road are signs—in particular, Cocoa's Trail to Great Brook.

Turn right to follow a peaceful path along the brook. Cascades dance in the sunlight. Across the brook are more stone walls. In one spot the water has carved a channel between large rocks, opposite which are the remains of what may have been a mill powered by the

What a fine place this must have been for Sunday visits and dooryard calls.

water here. Proceed past Hayes Farm (now reverted to forest) to reach the trail signs from which you started. Turn left to cross the stepping-stone brook and the rickety bridge. Pass the tumbledown shacks again and the carpet of myrtle on the path leading back to your car.

Part 2. There's a sign just as you come out to the road in front of the cellar holes at the top of the hill. It says "Wolf Tree Trail" and "Hilltop View." Just down the road to your left is a big sign that describes some fine old trees you will see if you take this part of the walk.

Pass the sign, which tells you that the old trees were planted to shade the cows and were called Wolf Trees because they wolfed sunlight and water from nearby seedlings.

You'll soon come to the Morgan Pasture sign. Bear left through a small but lovely woods, dense with spruces and white pines growing out of a bright green moss floor. A giant beech on your left stretches its myriad limbs to the sky.

Glacial erratic boulders sit by the side of the trail. The whole way up here you'll catch sight in the woods of the ghostly hulks of those wolf trees, relegated now to history, along with the first Bunkers.

Pass through another stone wall and a large flat rock tempting you to sit for a spell. Instead, keep on uphill and left through a wall with large quartz rocks in it. The blazes will then lead you to your right, up a narrow path carved through a great field full of juniper, to the last trail sign at the edge of the field, which is bordered by a wall. Notice the thorn-apple trees. You have a view for miles around you, across the hills to Mount Sunapee, down to King Ridge, beyond to the Mink Hills, and over to a shoulder of Mount Kearsarge.

After you've enjoyed all this, return to the cellar holes the way you came, and follow the return directions from there as in Part 1.

29. The Cascades

Walking distance: 3 miles
Walking time: 3 hours
New London, New Hampshire

THIS IS A LOVELY WOODLAND WALK, WHETHER
you stop at the Lower Cascades or make the entire trip. The pond
beyond the Upper Cascades gives you a peaceful vista and a quiet
retreat.

ACCESS

At the corner of Main and Pleasant Streets in New London, turn onto
Pleasant Street and pass the Kidder Building, a large yellow clapboard
house on your left. Travel 1.9 miles, past Pleasant Lake Inn on your
left and Pleasant Lake on your right, and around a curve to the left
to Pingree Road, which forks left. Go .5 mile on Pingree Road. You'll
pass a Cape Cod–style house on the left with a sign that indicates that
this was the home of Jeremiah Pingree, a farmer who came to New
London from eastern Massachusetts in 1792. Just past the farm, on
the right, is the Hayes Woods barricade. Park here and walk around
the barricade to begin a pleasant ramble.

TRAIL

Almost immediately a trail sign points left. The trail enters the woods
past a fallen tree, and goes through a blanket of myrtle on the ground.
A little farther on there are some fallen-in shacks off to the right of
the trail. Behind them and above the brook are the foundations of
what could have been Nathaniel Bunker's sawmill (see walk 28). Back
on the trail, a few steps will bring you to a bridge across Great Brook,
and then trail signs direct you to the Lower Cascades and the Bunker
Place (see "The Bunker Place" walk in this book). Turn left toward
the Lower Cascades and walk along the brook. You'll find that the
entire trail is well blazed with orange patches of paint on the trees.
Be sure to follow the blazes.

114

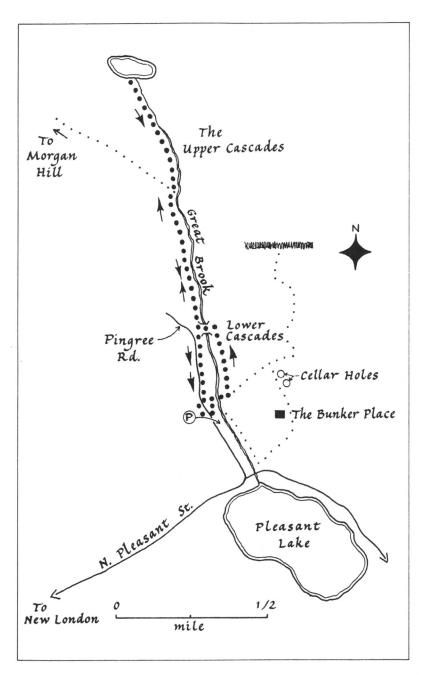

To Morgan Hill

The Upper Cascades

Great Brook

N

Lower Cascades

Pingree Rd.

P

Cellar Holes

The Bunker Place

N. Pleasant St.

Pleasant Lake

To New London

0   1/2
        mile

You'll soon cross a field full of ferns and berries under a power line, and then re-enter the woods. In midsummer a lone Indian pipe may poke its way into the middle of the path, or a yellow-and-brown-striped garter snake might slither in front of you and disappear under red-berried elder by the wayside.

Ten minutes of easy walking brings you to a fireplace you may use if you have a permit. Just beyond the fireplace the Lower Cascades run beneath another bridge and tumble over long, grey ledges. If the water is not too high, these rocks invite you to picnic or just to sit and muse on their flat tops. If it's a warm day take off your shoes and let the rushing water swirl around your ankles. Then cross the bridge and walk up a small hill to the road. If this is as far as you're going, turn left for a short walk down the old road to your car.

To continue to the Upper Cascades and the pond, turn right onto the road. You will come to a fork in the road; keep to the right over a rickety little wooden bridge across another brook. The road here looks less traveled. It once led to the farm you'll soon pass, which may have belonged to the Morgan family. The woods on either side of you were the family's pastures. Jonathan Morgan, a ship's captain who tired of life at sea, settled here to farm. It's difficult to imagine cattle grazing in what is now fairly dense forest. On your right, up a slight hill, stone walls still enclose a yard filled with raspberries. Day-lilies grow in the far corner of what must have been the dooryard. There are daisies and pink mallow. A building has fallen in. Black-eyed Susan and yarrow bloom across the road beneath taller meadow-sweet. A chestnut-sided warbler sings in a beech tree.

A little over .5 mile from the Lower Cascades bridge, junction signs point to Morgan Hill and to the Upper Cascades. Bear right for the cascades. You'll leave the brook for a while and may wonder if you're still on the trail. It does wind back again, through some muddy spots where you might see moose tracks. In about fifteen minutes you'll reach the Upper Cascades, the long ledges down which clear water plunges into Great Brook. The trail up the side of the cascades to the pond is well blazed but narrow and windy. In less than ten minutes you'll arrive at an opening and see the pond through the trees.

On the shore of the pond there's a wide rock to lunch on while you watch sparkling waters trickle through a long beaver dam. Beyond the dam, on the left side of the pond, you can see the beaver lodge— a big specimen.

Don't be in a hurry here. This is a place to spend some time with a camera. The little yellow-rumped myrtle warblers may entertain you at lunch, or a bullfrog might plunk on his banjo. You might see moose tracks in the mud here, headed for paths through the leatherleaf bushes that frame the pond. Sweet Gale bushes perfume the air around you. Sphagnum moss and dense bushes tell you that this pond has commenced on its trek back to being a woodland some day.

The Lower Cascades tumbles over long grey ledges.

30. The Philbrick-Cricenti Bog

Walking distance: 1 mile
Walking time: ½–1 hour
New London, New Hampshire

IN TOWNS THROUGHOUT NEW ENGLAND CONSER-
vation commissions work to save unique ecological areas for future
generations to study and enjoy. New London's commission has been
particularly successful in accomplishing its mission. The land now
designated the Philbrick-Cricenti Bog was acquired after twenty-five
years of hard work by the town commission, the two families whose
names it bears, the James Cleveland family, and the Federal Bureau
of Outdoor Recreation. This bog provides us with a remarkable opportunity to observe the process of lake-to-forest succession.

Lakes, left to natural forces, eventually return to land, but most
succeed from lake to wetland to marsh to woodland, or grassland,
without ever passing through the bog stage. A bog is formed when a
cold lake is colonized by the acidic sphagnum moss. Floating outward
from the shore, the moss eventually covers the lake's surface with a
self-perpetuating mat that disappears only when the water drains away
or is displaced by solid peat. In the process, it creates a base on which
various plants, shrubs, trees, and finally a climax forest take root. In
the Philbrick-Cricenti Bog, you see nearly all of these stages of succession.

ACCESS

Take the Newport Road .3 mile west of the Cricenti Shopping Center
(NH 11 westward from New London toward Georges Mills), or drive
east from Exit 12 of I-89. The entrance to this walk is from a wide
shoulder on the road, where you can park. There is no sign until you
get a few feet into the trail to the bog. Soon after you start you'll
reach a box containing maps that describe the area.

TRAIL

When the last glacier retreated, between ten and fourteen thousand

118

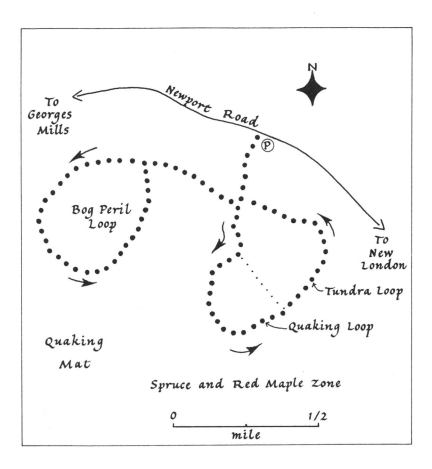

To
Georges
Mills

Newport Road

N

Ⓟ

To
New
London

Bog Peril
Loop

Tundra Loop

Quaking Loop

Quaking
Mat

Spruce and Red Maple Zone

0   1/2
          mile

years ago, it left a lake here. As you come down to its basin, you'll walk past the royal ferns and red maples that have grown onto the mat that claimed the open water. Where the underlying water is more acidic, cinnamon ferns replace the royal ferns, and black spruces outnumber maples.

You travel through the bog on wooden planks, which have been placed there so you won't sink through the mat. Notice the sphagnum moss and grasslike sedge, the first plants to move in over the pond. Feathery tamarack trees grow along the bog's edge. Dwarf trees have taken root on the mat. A great display of pitcher plant, which traps insects, grows on the open bog. Pitcher plant looks like antique car-

119

A boardwalk snakes across the bog's tundra landscape.

nival glass, and in June displays a tall, maroon-colored flower bending over its hollow leaves.

Beside the boardwalk grow dark green leatherleaf bushes, hung with white, bell-like flowers in early spring. There's also blue-green bog rosemary, and pale pink cranberry blossoms hug the ground. The laurel has pink blooms in late June. Although the mat is soggy underfoot and you can feel the plank walks bounce beneath you, it's still hard to imagine that just one hundred years ago people fished on open water here.

As you approach the edge of the old lake shore, you reach the forest that will someday take over the entire bog. Now you're back in more familiar-looking territory, among birch trees and spruces, with goldthread and Canada mayflower on the forest floor. You come out of the woods over a moss-covered log bound by the roots of younger trees. If you're exploring the bog in June, don't miss the white calla growing on both sides of the trail here. These flowers, like the pitcher plant, are peculiar to bogs and pond edges, and are a special treat.

Follow the area map to the Bog Peril Loop to see the tundra landscape. Be sure to stay on the walk, for this loop is well named: you could sink into it quite easily. Animals have drowned here.

Every week and each season bring exciting changes in the bog. The walk is so full of beauty and information that the mile seems short indeed.

31. Lucia's Lookout

Walking distance: 6 miles
Walking time: 5 hours
Pillsbury State Park—Washington, New Hampshire

PILLSBURY STATE PARK, A WILDERNESS AREA OF
over 5,000 acres, was originally a 2,400 acre tract of land, donated to
the state in 1920 by Albert E. Pillsbury, one of the founders of the
Society for the Protection of New Hampshire Forests. It was designated a state park in 1952. Before then it was a forest preserve and a
biological experiment area. It was off-and-on a mill town and farmland. It was also a lumbering town, boasting its own post office, and
was known as Cherry Valley, New Hampshire. Previous to all this it
was virgin forest and hunting grounds of the Squakheag Indians. Its
brooks and nine of its ten ponds are headwaters of the Ashuelot River.

Lucia's Lookout, to which this walk will take you, was named by
an Appalachian Mountain Club trail crew as a surprise for Lucia
Kittredge, who in 1974 worked with them as a student intern for the
Society for the Protection of New Hampshire Forests. Their job was
to reroute the part of the old Monadnock-Sunapee Greenway that goes
from Pillsbury State Park to its northern terminus on Mount Sunapee.
They acquired easements from private property owners, and rights-
of-way so that the trail could be brought up from the lowlands to the
heights of land and the ridge on which we find the lookout.

The Monadnock-Sunapee Greenway offers many opportunities for
day hikes or two- to three-day trips along its length. You can also use
it to connect with the Metacomet-Monadnock Trail, on which you
can walk all the way from Connecticut to Mount Monadnock. For
Monadnock-Sunapee Greenway information, call or write to The Society for the Protection of New Hampshire Forests, Concord, New
Hampshire 03301. For a guide to the Metacomet-Monadnock Trail,
write to the Appalachian Mountain Club, 5 Joy Street, Boston, MA
02108.

The walk to Lucia's Lookout is a long one, with sylvan views, forest
ponds, and rocky ledges high above Pillsbury State Park. It can also
be a short walk to sit beside one of the ponds or brooks you'll find

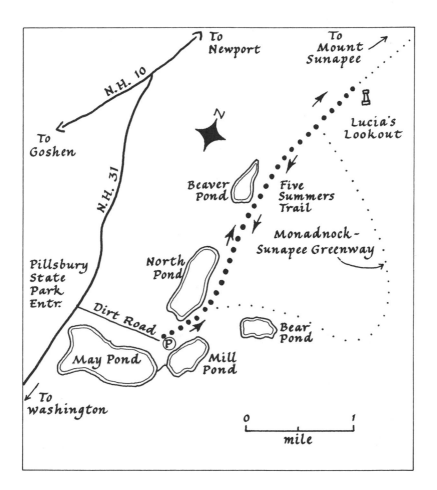

along the way, enjoy the wildflowers and the birds, budded spring trees, or bright fall colors.

ACCESS

Drive to Pillsbury State Park, which is on NH 31 halfway between the picturesque village of Washington and the junction of NH 10 and NH 31, .6 mile south of Goshen. Enter the park and travel straight up a dirt road, past May Pond on your right, to a picnic area with children's swings. Mill Pond lies directly ahead of you. Park here and

123

walk up the road to your left. A sign on a tree reads "Five Summers Trail." Your way is clearly marked by blue blazes on trees and rocks.

TRAIL

Drive or walk up the dirt road past the trail sign. In about 15 minutes, you will reach a wide road on your right. In season, it has signs that point to Bear Pond and the Monadnock-Sunapee Greenway. Pass this road and park on the left-hand side of the road you are on. Then walk straight ahead on the Five Summers Trail, being sure to follow the blue blazes.* As you amble along the road a view of North Pond opens up on your left. In the spring delicate white blossoms on hobblebush decorate the roadside. You'll see purple trillium, yellow clintonia, and Canada mayflower, too. In midsummer blue pickerelweed pokes its spike above the pond's surface, where fragrant white water lilies float. Turtlehead and orange jewelweed blossom beside the road.

About 2 miles down the trail, sharply pointed sticks in a clearing on the left indicate that beavers have been busy here. There's a small dam they've built in a stream. Meadowsweet and deep pink steeple-bush bloom along the stream's edge. Goldenrod shows its yellow head in August. You'll cross a wide wooden bridge. Much of this walk takes you along logging roads cut by the International Paper Company, and you'll see evidence of their work.

Blackberries grow along the roadside as you start uphill. A tree on the right has three fresh, oblong holes where the pileated woodpecker has hammered. In five minutes you'll come to another bridge across a cascading stream. The road continues uphill, then levels out along a big beaver pond. On a foggy day, you'll gaze beyond the leatherleaf bushes along the shore to see the ghostly skeletons of trees where there was once forest. Evergreens soon appear in the woods that your trail runs through. It appears that the loggers left off here so that you could enjoy a woodland path for the rest of the trip.

Two blazes at a fork in the trail are your signal to bear right soon, and in five minutes another two blazes tell you to bear left onto an uphill trail. Rocks begin to show in the trail and on both sides of it. You wind past moss-covered boulders to a sign-marked junction of

*At the time of writing, logging operations were underway on the upper portion of the Five Summers Trail. Walkers should ask at the office at the park entrance whether this trail is still usable, or whether it is advisable to take the longer route via the Monadnock-Sunapee Greenway (see map).

You can see down to the ponds and lakes you start from and the wooded hills that surround them.

the Monadnock-Sunapee and Five Summers trails. You are 3.9 miles from the sign on the tree at the beginning of your walk.

From here on the blazes are the white blaze of the Monadnock-Sunapee Greenway. There remains only about ten minutes of steeply uphill trail over rock ledges to the wide clearing called Lucia's Lookout. These last few minutes of hard work earn you a respite. Lunch in the clearing on a nice day affords views over the park and down to the ponds below. The trail continues 3.3 miles to Mount Sunapee's summit.

The entire Monadnock-Sunapee Greenway is 47 miles long, and there are campsites along it. The ridge between Lucia's Lookout and the top of Mount Sunapee provides an especially fine walk. Maps of the entire trail are available from the Society for the Protection of New Hampshire Forests.

You can return to your car the way you came, or you can make a 7.1-mile loop if you're feeling ambitious. From the junction of the Monadnock-Sunapee and Five Summers trails, turn left and follow the white blazes for 3 miles to the Bear Pond Trail junction. Turn right and follow this trail until it meets a logging road with a sign that directs you to Pillsbury State Park. This road takes you downhill about 1 mile, past Bear Pond, and out onto the road near where you started on the trail. Turn left and walk about half a mile to your car.

32. Bear Pond Beaver Dam

Walking distance: 2 miles
Walking time: 1 hour
Pillsbury State Park—Washington, New Hampshire

BEAVERS ARE NATURE'S FANTASTIC ENGINEERS. Their dams not only create deep ponds on which they build their own homes, but provide natural habitats for fish and birds. They also help to prevent floods. Because beavers' principal food is bark and twigs, they prefer to live in small bodies of water surrounded by many trees. They don't protect themselves by fighting, but seek safety in the water. Beavers enter their lodges by underwater tunnels. If a body of water is not deep enough for the beavers to build a lodge upon, they first build a dam to deepen it. Boughs, logs, stones, and mud go into the construction of a dam. All members of a beaver colony work together, gnawing down trees, cutting them up with their sharp teeth, and then dragging or floating the pieces to where they're needed. The logs arc laid in place and empty spaces filled in, first with boughs and twigs, then with a mud plaster. The dams are sturdy enough to hold back water for many years, and feel as firm as any bridge to walk upon.

In Pillsbury State Park you can walk to a beaver dam, examine it, and wonder at these marvelous animals. You probably won't see the beavers themselves, because they usually work at night.

ACCESS

Pillsbury State Park is on NH 31, halfway between the village of Washington and the junction of NH 10 and NH 31, .6 mile south of Goshen. Turn into the park at the entrance sign and travel along the dirt road past May Pond to Mill Pond, where there are picnic tables and children's swings. Park here to begin your walk.

TRAIL

Walk up the road that leads to the left from Mill Pond, past a sign that says "Five Summers Trail," to cross a brook and in about half

127

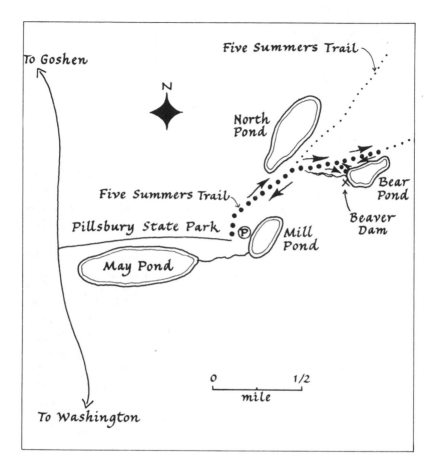

To Goshen

N

Five Summers Trail

North
Pond

Bear
Pond

Five Summers Trail

Beaver
Dam

Pillsbury State Park

Mill
Pond

May Pond

0   1/2
       mile

To Washington

a mile reach a right-hand turn onto an old road to Bear Pond. The road is grassy and overgrown. It's often muddy, and you may see deer tracks or little tree frogs leaping in front of you. Where the road forks, keep left. In less than half a mile you reach a wide brook full of rocks. Immediately past the brook, before some high ledges, a narrow fishermen's trail goes right along the brook, and steeply uphill. You pass some nice cascades and two small pools, and then you're at the beaver dam. It's overgrown with bushes and trees on it as tall as you are. The lodges don't seem to be in sight, but perhaps you can find them. The dam is enormous, an awe-inspiring feat of engineering.

128

When you return to the road, turn right and go a little farther to more views of Bear Pond. Here you'll see old trees bleaching in the sun, with what appear to be Osprey nests in their tops. The shore is bordered with grasses and leatherleaf bushes. Fish jump now and then. In the late spring you may hear a frog glee club, or even two, singing to each other across the pond in their deep, guttural voices.

Usually beavers work at night, but sometimes. . . .

33. The Newbury Cut

Walking distance: 5 miles
Walking time: 2 hours
South Newbury, New Hampshire

AS YOU STROLL ALONG THIS FORMER RAILROAD
bed, which is now a lane shaded by birches, green-leaved in the
summer and yellow in the fall, picture yourself in high-buttoned shoes
and long skirts, or a stiff collar and a derby hat, riding behind a
puffing steam engine to a holiday on Sunapee Lake.

The Civil War created a great demand for consumer goods made
in New Hampshire's factories and produce grown on New Hampshire's farms, and the trains were the most practical way to deliver
the products. Tourism became popular. Railroads, therefore, boomed
in mid-nineteenth century New Hampshire, which came to be called
"The Railroad State." Nearly every town had its own railroad. By
1851, the Concord and Contoocook Valley Railroad was being encouraged to extend its lines to Claremont (the western end of the line
was then at Bradford). By the spring of 1866, all the towns from
Concord to Claremont had voted funds for the expansion. A great
ground-breaking ceremony took place in Newport on June 3, 1870,
and the job moved along quickly until the line reached Newbury.
Here a massive wall of granite, far too steep to be graded, stopped
the work.

Contractors commenced blasting in August. Employing a new kind
of steam drill with a 2½-inch bit, they crept forward nine feet every
fifty minutes. Ten-pound charges of black powder blasted the rock
to sizes suitable for fill. The following spring when newspaper editors
were invited to see the blasting, six quarts of nitroglycerin were used
to blast seventy to eighty cubic feet of stone. A final blast, on September 11, 1871, finished the "Newbury Cut," which was considered
one of the great feats of railroad enterprise.

For ninety years the Concord and Claremont was a boon to merchants and the tourist trade. A tourist party took the last passenger
ride in 1961 in an attempt to renew interest in the fun of train travel,

130

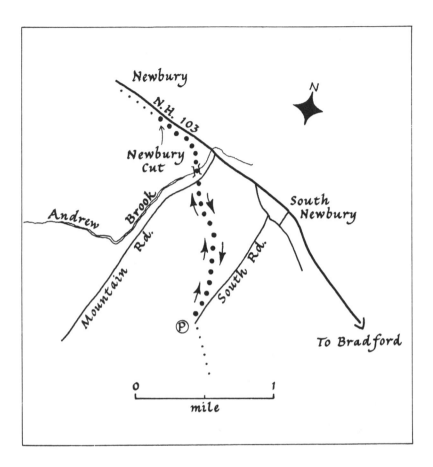

but unfortunately, the idea died: the locomotive engine could not pass safety inspections.

ACCESS

From NH 103, 3 miles northwest of Bradford and 3 miles southeast of Newbury, signs direct you to South Newbury. Drive into the village to South Road and travel south exactly 1 mile. You will pass a red house on your right, and then two white Cape Cod–style houses close to the road, also on your right. Then you'll see the old railroad bed on both the right and left-hand sides of the road. Your walk begins on the right, toward Newbury. You can park your car up the hill a

Great granite ledges rise above you . . . you can almost hear the train chug laboriously through this height-of-land.

bit, on the wide shoulder of the road, and walk back to commence your journey into bygone times.

TRAIL

The railroad bed climbs very gradually. You cross old bridges and follow old stone walls that in the days of the trains delineated farms and pastures. There must have been views of the surrounding hills in those times, before birches and beeches and maples grew up to obscure them. Purple flowering raspberry blooms along one wall. Andrew Brook runs through a culvert under a steep grade.

Imagine suspendered men toiling with hand shovels to push the railroad west from here, and baggage cars piled high with the effects of vacationing families up from Boston for the summer.

You cross Mountain Road 1¾ miles from the start. Fifteen more minutes of poking along brings you suddenly into the historic cut. Great granite ledges rise above you. Horsehair lichen hangs in strings from the rocks. Chips of mica sparkle and flash. You can almost hear the train chug laboriously over this height of land.

Go back the way you came, and on the return trip notice the glacial erratic boulders that run east and west, almost in a line, about 2 miles south of the cut. At this point the mountain called Bald Sunapee appears, rising above you across the trail. Ten minutes farther on, a dirt road slants across yours. On a hot day in midsummer walk right up this road a piece to refresh yourself with the sugar-sweet blackberries growing in abundance on either side of you. Then turn around and finish your walk the way you came in.

Should you not want to walk this far, the Newbury Cut can be reached more easily from Newbury. Park your car at the public dock; the trail begins behind the mall across the street. A ten-minute walk through the young birch woods will bring you to the historic cut.

The railroad bed makes an easy ski tour.

34. The Cheese Factory Trail

Walking distance: 1 mile
Walking time: 40 minutes
Grafton, Vermont

THE VILLAGE OF GRAFTON, FOUNDED IN 1754, IS A
jewel—shaded streets and well-kept old houses, baskets of geraniums
hanging from the hospitable white clapboard tavern. One hundred
and fifty years ago this was a thriving community of 1,500 farmers,
artisans, merchants, and professionals. The Saxtons River, which

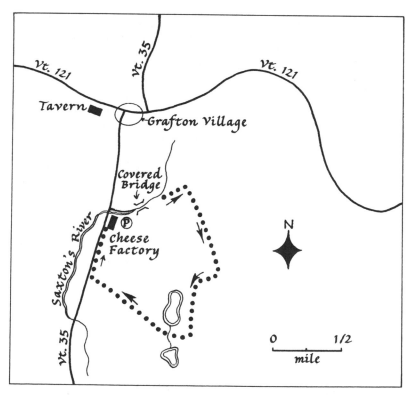

Turn left beyond the covered bridge.

flows through Grafton, once had six dams furnishing water to more than a dozen mills between Grafton and Cambridgeport. The Serpentine Rock, which you can walk to, contained the largest deposit of serpentine on the North American Continent. Two of the largest soapstone quarries in the United States are located here.

The Grafton Historical Society has published a guide to nine local walks that take you to sites of historical significance.

The walk we chose is a small one. It starts from the cheese factory, where you can buy snacks to take along on your walk. You can return later to take home a choice of several varieties of mouth-watering local cheeses.

ACCESS

From Bellows Falls, Vermont, drive northwest on VT 121 to Grafton. The Tavern is on the southwest corner where VT 121 and VT 35 meet. Turn left onto VT 35 and you'll quickly reach the cheese factory on your left. It's an easy walk from the center of town, or you can park at the trailhead. Your walk begins at the covered bridge at the cheese factory.

TRAIL

Cross the river via the covered bridge, and walk across a meadow full of late summer asters and goldenrod. Turn right up a gentle hill and you will soon come to a junction with a wooded path. There are tiny lance-leaved asters with purple centers along the trail, and a bank of spectacular rust-colored ferns. Stone gateposts stand in front of a tumbled-down house. At a trail junction with signs, bear right to the ponds. Turn left over a wooden bridge to follow the trail along the first pond, and then cross a tiny bridge over the pond's outlet. The second pond is across the field to the left. You're in the middle of a cross-country ski center—its office is the cabin by the first pond. Wander toward the stone wall and the road. Turn right and walk back along the road, beside the wall, to the cheese factory.

Stop in the village at the museum, or at the little store, for the Historical Society's directions for the other walks out of Grafton. They range in distance from 1 mile to about 5, beginning at the library. Come back in the wintertime to enjoy the ski trails.

Bellows Falls
South to
Massachusetts

35. High Blue

Walking distance: 1½ miles
Walking time: 1 hour
Walpole, New Hampshire

IN 1981 THE SOCIETY FOR THE PROTECTION OF NEW
Hampshire Forests received, by bequest from Stephen Warner of
Malibu, California, the parcel of land he knew as "High Blue." It
came with the request that the public be allowed to enjoy it, as he
had, for picnicking and relaxation. The Society has therefore set aside
this property forever for you and your descendents.

As the property name suggests, superb views of the Connecticut
River Valley and the Green Mountains unfold from high ledges you
can easily reach. The hay fields, on either side of the old Scovill Road,
are maintained and harvested by a local farmer.

ACCESS

A scenic ride over high land and low, past old houses and farmland,
brings you to the Warner Forest. From Keene follow NH 12A north
from NH 12 for just under 1 mile. Turn left onto Old Walpole Road.
Watch for the Walpole-Surry town line at approximately 5 miles. At
about 1.2 miles beyond the town line, turn right onto unmarked
Crehore Road and then left at .2 mile at a T. In .3 mile after the T
turn right onto also unmarked Scovill Road and follow it approximately .7 mile; it bears around to the left at a fork. Your trail begins
where a sign to Warner Forest stands on the left and a field opens up
beyond the woods, on your right. You can park at the sign.

TRAIL

Follow the old road into the woods and then out onto the farmer's
field, bordered by beech woods and raspberries. You'll see lots of
flowers in May. The woods are blanketed with bellwort, Canada mayflower, and wild oats. Go around the gate at the end of the field and
continue up a very gradual hill, past lichen-covered rocks to a fork

138

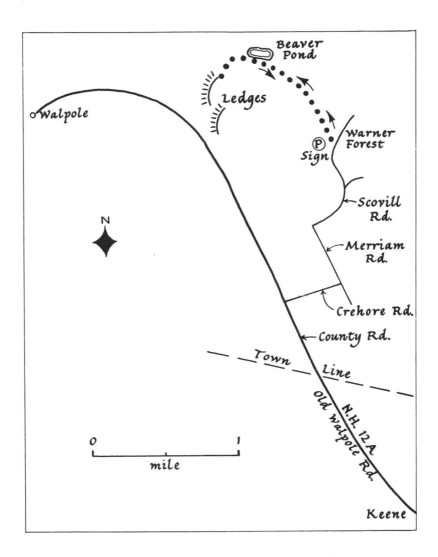

in the path. Bear left. An old chimney has tumbled down and an elderberry bush hangs over it: did whoever lived here make elderberry wine or jelly?

The stone wall you pass through reminds you that this forest was once pasture. Do you ever think of our ancestors who cleared the trees to make farms, and then, when the land proved to be marginally productive, left it to grow back to what it is today? This was the story

139

Lunch in the sun on the ledges.

of New Hampshire, over and over again. Some of the original farmers moved to mill towns and city factories during the Industrial Revolution. Some moved west to better agricultural territory.

There are violets in the path and then a tiny pond, built by beavers. Their dam is off to your right below a great outcropping of white quartz. When you come to an open space at the top of the rise, turn left. You'll see a stone cairn on a rock off the path and into the woods. Above it are some flat ledges where you can sit in the sun with your picnic or a good book.

The Connecticut River Valley is over the treetops in the distance. Rolling Vermont hills and then the mountains rise beyond the river.

On your way back, as you near the gate, look up to see Mount Monadnock's silhouette in the distance.

Return to your car, and when you reach the County Road turn right and continue down to picturesque Walpole. As of this writing you can still buy an ice cream cone there for thirty-five cents.

36. A Walk Around Historic Walpole

Walking distance: about 1 mile
Walking time: 1–2 hours
Walpole, New Hampshire

A WALK AROUND HISTORIC WALPOLE IS WELL worth your while, for the town is a unique example of an early Connecticut River Valley settlement. Although its earliest lodgings, Indian wigwams and log cabins, are long gone, many of its first houses have been blessed with longevity and excellent preservation. The lovely old homes are still inhabited, many by descendants of the original white settlers.

In 1724, when England claimed ownership of American land, royal Governor Benning Wentworth hired Colonel Benjamin Bellows to survey, in the interest of development, the Connecticut River Valley north of Vernon, in what is now Vermont, just north of the present Massachusetts border. Governor Wentworth granted Colonel Bellows six square miles to develop into a town.

The area was all forest, inhabited sporadically by Indians who came to fish and hunt. The first white settler was John Kilburn, who held New York title to the land. However, because Kilburn's title was not from the King, it was worthless, and Colonel Bellows was free to develop his grant. In 1752 Colonel Bellows received a royal charter and officially established what was called Bellowstown until 1761, when, loyalties to the "mother country" becoming shaky, many New England towns were renamed for important British personages in an attempt to bolster patriotism for the motherland. Sir Robert Walpole, England's first Prime Minister, was honored with a renaming of the town we know as Walpole.

Colonel Bellows cleared his land for farming, which has remained the mainstay of this fertile valley's economy. There was also excellent fishing and hunting along the river. Trees from the virgin forests were floated down the river to become masts for ships in the English Navy.

141

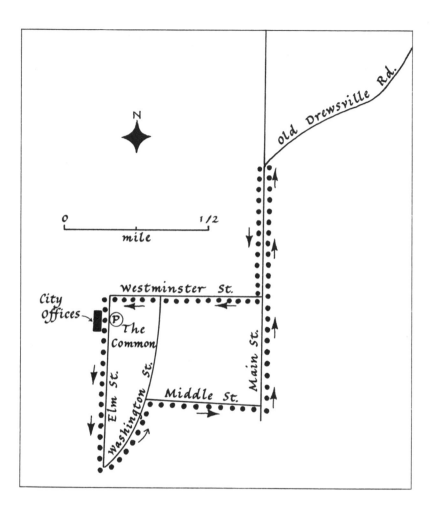

Local farmers through the years have produced corn, wheat, rye, hay, peas, beans, potatoes, maple sugar, milk, butter, cheese and tobacco. They've raised horses, cattle, sheep, and pigs. In the times before lower tariffs made it economical to import British woolens, they sold wool. The Hubbard Farm, still active, is world renowned for its chickens. At one time Walpole was the country's largest producer of corn. The area became and remains prosperous.

When Walpole, or Bellowstown, was first settled, communication with more settled parts of New England was mainly by boat from

142

Hartford, but boats could not get beyond Bellows Falls. Eventually stagecoaches and railroads replaced river traffic.

Colonel Bellows was a hardworking and valuable citizen. The town of Bellows Falls was named after him in appreciation of his service in many important civic positions there. He and his wife had four sons, and there are still five Bellows houses in Walpole. There were at one time fourteen one-room schoolhouses, and for a while the town's population was greater than Keene's.

Walpole was owned by England until our War of Independence. The first casualty of that war took place when a Mr. French was shot in the town of Westminster, Vermont, directly across the river. One month later the ruckus in Concord, Massachusetts took place and our revolution began in earnest.

ACCESS

From Brattleboro travel north on I-91 to Bellows Falls, and then south on NH 12. From Keene travel north on NH 12. From Hanover or Claremont travel south on NH 12A, and then south on NH 12 to Walpole.

TRAIL

Begin your walk at the Congregational Church (the oldest church building in town) on the common at Washington Street. The church stands on property given in 1833 by Abigail Richardson, whose gift stipulated that she expected "to have a good pew, rent free" as long as she lived. Walk north to Westminster Street. Directly across the street is a brick home which belongs to Mr. and Mrs. Guy Bemis. Mr. Bemis is known as the unofficial town historian. He knows a wealth of fascinating details concerning the history of not only Walpole, but the entire river valley. He's restored many of the old houses here. His own home includes five fireplaces, a brick oven, and the original Indian shutters. Next door to the Bemises is the former home, built in 1818, of a granddaughter of Benjamin Bellows.

Turn left at the corner onto Elm Street. Pass the Catholic Church, built in 1845. Methodists owned the building in 1848; they sold it to the Episcopalians in 1868, and in 1873 the Episcopalians sold it to Catholics.

Move on to the square colonial house built in 1806. It was once

143

used for a clothing shop; at another time it served as a parsonage for the Congregational Church across the common. You probably know that commons were so named because they were shared, or common pasture for local animals. Picket fences once surrounded houses you see to protect them from straying cattle and sheep.

A large house with a long porch and covered balcony, built in 1812, has served as an inn off-and-on through the years. It contains rare French scenic wallpaper and fine paneling. James Michener once stayed at the inn here. He used Walpole as his missionaries' departure point to the Pacific in his novel *Hawaii*.

Cross the common to Middle Street, which intersects Main Street. On the corner of Middle and Washington Streets is the Congregational parsonage, built in or around 1798 for Micanor Townsley, a cabinet-maker. It's been a parsonage since 1883.

Beyond the parsonage there's a house, built in 1793, which has a secret closet once used to conceal runaway slaves from the South. On the opposite corner of Middle and Main Streets stands a house built in 1786 as a square colonial, but which, you will notice, underwent quite a change during the Greek Revival period in American architecture.

Northward and east of Main Street, up the hill, you come to the Old Academy building, built in 1831 as a private school. It later became the public high school, and in 1951 was converted to the museum for the Walpole Historical Society. It is now designated a National Historic Place.

Two houses north of here, on Main Street, Benjamin Bellows's son built a home in 1794 as a wedding gift for his daughter. Teenaged Louisa May Alcott lived in this house for a time with her aunt. A lilac hedge on County Road was reputed to have inspired her novel *Underneath the Lilacs*.

The gray building just past the Pizza Parlor was once a print shop, and a bit north, across the street, a white house with a curved front roof and three dormers is probably the oldest house in the village. Built in 1762, the house retains some of the original plaster on the interior walls, horizontal wide board panels, and magnificent chestnut floors.

Back on the other side of the street, a house built in 1794 was once the Johnson Tavern. Dr. Ebenezer Morse established his medical practice here in 1813. He was also a historian and a fiddler, and he wrote rhymes about the joys of country living. He is reputed to have handed out bread pills to his patients.

You could finish your walk here or continue up the hill as far as Old Drewsville Road, past many other lovely houses. The large Victorian house with a cupola was originally owned by a wealthy manufacturer, who embellished it with silver doorknobs and a spiral staircase. The cupola had a blue ceiling with white clouds.

Josiah Bellows III built his house just north of here in about 1813. Walpole's first school, one of three schools built in 1770, stood nearby. Bricks used to be made across the street, down by the brook. Just before you bear right onto Old Drewsville Road is another Bellows house, where the first meeting house stood.

You can get in your car and travel Old Drewsville Road, which takes a lovely course through the woods, down to Blanchard Brook, then walk westward along the brook to Blanchard's Falls, where Colonel Bellows set up his first saw and grist mill in 1795. There were five mills in town at that time.

Today's Walpole supports two farm machine distributors and the Hubbard Poultry Farms.

If you become entranced, as we did, with this beautiful town, and would like to stay a while, The Homestead Inn and four Bed and Breakfast houses offer lodgings. On Westminster Street there's an old-fashioned soda fountain where in 1988 you could buy an ice cream cone for thirty-five cents. Next door is a nice little restaurant. The golf club serves lunches on a wide porch that overlooks the valley, and the inn serves meals, too. There is a pizza parlor on Main Street, and a supermarket for picnic makings.

37. Ledges Overlook

Walking distance: 2 miles
Walking time: 1½ hours
Townshend Reservoir—Townshend, Vermont

YOU WILL FIND THE LEDGES OVERLOOK TRAIL
well named for its many ledges that overlook a lovely bit of the Vermont landscape. The trail, well maintained by the U.S. Army Corps
of Engineers, begins and ends on the west shore of the Townshend
Reservoir, between the towns of Townshend and West Townshend.
Gentle hills shelter the West River, which has been dammed to form
the reservoir on one side of the access road, and which cascades
through a gorge on the other side. There are shaded picnic areas and
a beach open to the public.

The Ledges Overlook Trail is not long, and provides a fine ramble
at any time of year.

ACCESS

Townshend lies 17 miles northwest of Brattleboro on VT 30. Continue
on VT 30 toward West Townshend and the reservoir. Turn left at
the reservoir to cross the dam and reach a small picnic area on the
right side of the road. Park here in the off-season, when the gate will
probably be closed. Walk past the beach to a large picnic area (about
one-half mile). You will soon see a small arrow on a sign, on a tree
to your right, that reads "trail." The orange blazes on the trees to
your left start you on your walk.

TRAIL

You'll quickly cross an overgrown road, and then an old wall that no
doubt once edged a pasture. Bear left up a long, gradual climb through
open woods of sturdy, mixed hardwoods and hemlocks. In about
twenty minutes the trail narrows and winds through a spectacular
growth of ferns that shelter the roots of yellow birches, hemlocks,
maples, and higher up, oaks. It's a long but easy uphill walk for

146

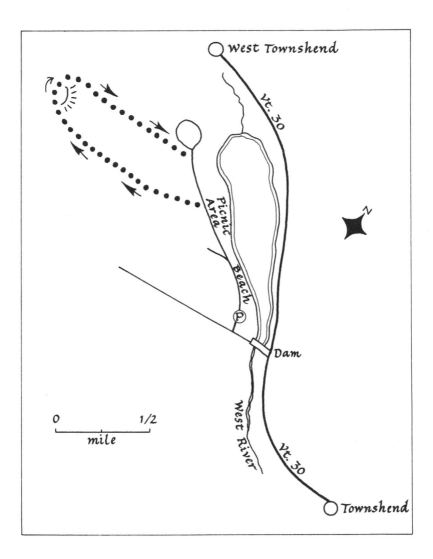

another fifteen minutes to a switchback that leads you further uphill. Now you can peer through the trees to the river below, and in a few moments, just past a large oak, see all the way down to the beach.

You'll come into a clearing and notice open ledges on your right. Take time to rest and enjoy a panorama of the reservoir, the dam, the Scott covered bridge, Bald Mountain, and the river.

Enjoy a panorama of the reservoir, the dam, Bald Mountain and the river.

From here the trail leads northwest and north up over the ledges and then across a ridge. Follow yellow blazes downhill for a while, and then reach more of the orange ones. You'll also see green and yellow Corps of Engineers blazes on some trees. The path downhill is gradual, too, and gives you ample opportunity to enjoy the woods and the songbirds. You circle around a great fallen beech tree. Yellowed ferns brighten the forest. Tiny orange newts crawl across the path in late summer.

The trail comes out of the woods across from the picnic area, about 400 feet up the road from where you started. Turn right and walk back to your car.

38. Horatio Colony Land Trust

Walking distance: about 3 miles
Walking time: about 4 hours
Keene, New Hampshire

HORATIO COLONY, A PARTNER IN THE FAULKNER-Colony Mills in Keene, spent many happy summers with his family on this property and in the home he built on its height of land. His grandson and heir, Horatio Colony, left over 450 acres of rich natural resource to the people of Keene and surrounding areas, to be enjoyed for generations to come. Students of Antioch, New England College have studied and documented, for all who explore here, the preserve's wealth of natural assets and history. Geologists will see examples of tremendous folding, underground volcanic activity, and the glacial forces of the Ice Age. Historians will find the cellar holes of early New England farmhouses. Naturalists will enjoy wildflowers, birds, and other animals, as well as rare trees and bushes.

This description of a walk through these woods will be only a sketch. A box at the trailhead contains copies of an excellent detailed chronicle organized for you by Antioch people. The estimated walking time above gives you opportunity to enjoy in depth the story of what has happened and is happening here. Although we are all welcome to enjoy the Colony Land Trust, please remember that you are a guest here and must respect the treasures that are being shared.

ACCESS

One mile west of the junction (and traffic lights) where NH 9 goes west from Keene, bear left and drive .3 mile past a chain gate on the left to a second gate on the left. You can park on the wide shoulder to the left of the road, and begin your walk here.

TRAIL

Start through the gate into a pine and hemlock forest. The path climbs uphill and soon crosses Old Daniels Hill Road to a framed map of

149

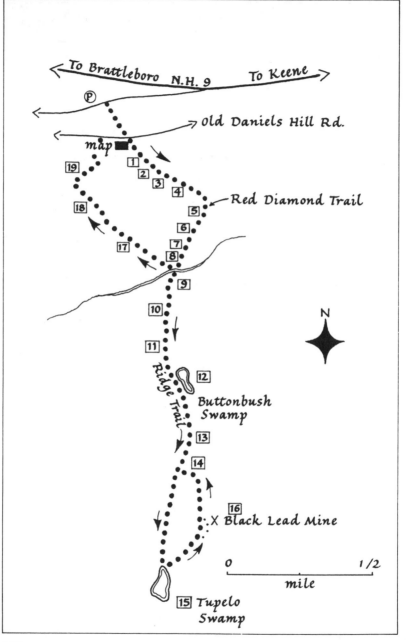

To Brattleboro N.H. 9 To Keene

P

Old Daniels Hill Rd.

map

19

1

2

3

4

Red Diamond Trail

5

18

6

7

17

8

9

10

11

Ridge Trail

12

Buttonbush Swamp

13

14

16

X Black Lead Mine

15 Tupelo Swamp

N

0   1/2
      mile

the preserve and a box holding the descriptive booklets for your walk. The Red Diamond Trail is well marked with diamond-shaped blazes on trees. The Ridgetop Trail is marked with light blue, oblong blazes. If your time is short or your stamina not too great, take the Red Diamond Trail around the short loop and enjoy part of the preserve. The hill on the Red Diamond trail is the hardest section of the walk, so if you can, you should allow yourself time to enjoy the rest, which is mostly pretty level going.

Leave southward from Old Daniels Hill Road and the map. Stone walls remind you once more that many of New Hampshire's forests were once cleared farmland. Now this one is overgrown with transitional forest (*transitional* means that there is a mix of trees from both northern and southern climates). Before springtime leaves on the trees shut out the sunlight, wildflowers bloom along the path. Red-eyed vireos, ovenbirds, and eastern wood pewees are some of the birds you'll hear in the spring. In the fall they move south in search of warmer weather and more abundant food.

Climb steadily uphill through the birch woods. At marked Site 3 a soil pit has been dug to show you the different layers of soil that constitute this land. The top layer is decaying plant and animal parts that fertilize the soil below. Next comes the topsoil, which is the most fertile part, and then the subsoil, composed of nutrients washed down from the first two. The bottom layer represents the parent material of non-living elements, in this case compacted gray sand.

Rocks begin to show as we move up West Hill. At Site 4 you see a common metamorphic rock called gneiss, which is quite resistant to erosion. The abundance of metamorphic rocks here have helped to preserve the hill. A little farther on, dark blue blazes on two trees indicate a short trail to the right, where you will see pegmatite ledges formed millions of years ago. Three minerals—quartz, mica, and feldspar—make up the pegmatite, which is the youngest rock on the preserve.

Ice Age glaciers all over New England left behind huge boulders, known as erratics because they are different from the local bedrock. Site 5 has a tall erratic boulder covered with juicy deer lichen, on which deer feed in the winter.

Now you reach the hilltop. There's a view of Keene beyond the foundation of Grandfather Horatio Colony's summer cabin. Built around the turn of this century, the cabin was enjoyed by family and friends for many years. From here on the walk is easy, with many exciting things to see and to learn about. You'll see dead and decaying logs blown down by the 1938 hurricane, and stumps from a recent logging operation. A fork in the road brings you to a cellar hole. In the 1800s Japhet Parker chose this site for his farm because of its good exposure to the sun, convenient water supply, and plowable land— hard to imagine now that it's all forest. In those early days many farmers cleared and settled this hill. Unfortunately, the land proved to be marginally fertile, and eventually the farmers moved on to earn their livings elsewhere.

The Red Diamond Trail leads downhill from here. Take the left fork to follow light blue markers onto the Ridgeline Trail to complete the longer walk. Almost immediately you will see two white birch trees covered with shelflike fungi known as polypores. These act as decomposers, breaking down wood to extract nutrients from it. Eventually the fungus decays and returns these nutrients to the soil. The dark brown, or tinder polypore was in former times soaked in kerosene and used to start fires. Dentists used its spongy tissues to fill teeth.

The great granitic rock formation standing on its edge at Site 11 is well worth a visit. You'll see intrusions into the granite of younger stripes of quartz. The granite's surface is covered with water-loving plants known as bryophytes, which have lived on the earth for 400 million years.

As you continue along the main trail you come to Buttonbush Swamp, formed years ago by beavers. In late fall there's a skim of ice on the water, dotted with snowflakes that sparkle in the sun. Look for red maples, royal ferns, and the round "button" of the buttonbush that grows out in the swamp. The trail now runs along a cascading brook. It crosses a small log bridge to Site 13, where there's a patch of leatherwood bushes. American Indians used the flexible branches of leatherwood to make thongs for their feet. The plant also served as a pain reliever for toothaches. Leatherwood grows in moist areas that are nutrient-rich.

A short walk past the leatherwood brings you to a quartzite ledge that rises high on your left. Tremendous forces of heat and pressure changed sandstone into the rose and smoky white splendor before you. Large boulders at the base of the ledge show you how the hard, brittle quartzite erodes by breaking off from the ledge face. There's a ramp you can climb up to see where a glacier polished the rock surface to shiny smoothness as it passed by here ten thousand years ago.

152

Black lead mined here made melting pots for copper foundries.

Return to the main trail to descend a long hill through a deep green hemlock forest. Shiny-leaved goldthread covers the forest floor. In June it bears minute white flowers. You soon reach a junction and signs to the Tupelo Swamp and the Lead Mine. Go toward Tupelo Swamp. There you'll be rewarded with a nice little pond that is the swamp and the Tupelo Trees, which are of southern ancestry. It's a natural mystery how they came to New Hampshire, and how they have survived here. Tracks of deer, mink, weasel, and snowshoe hare mark the soil near the water.

Follow the path back to the north. Take a fork to the right and go uphill to the water-filled hole that was once part of the lead mine. Climb up the ledge on your left to a clearing and stop a while for lunch. The black lead extracted from the earth here made melting pots for copper foundries. A declining economy after the Civil War rendered mining impractical in this region.

Enjoy a leisurely walk back to the trail junction, and turn left past Japhet Parker's cellar hole. Site 17 is the deer yard. Hemlocks protect it in the winter, providing shelter for the animals. The trees also allow sunlight to penetrate through their lacy branches to the ground.

Farther down the path, at Site 18, there's a large, standing, dead tree, called a snag. Pileated woodpeckers have made large holes in the trunk in their search for insects. The holes make good nesting places for other birds. At Site 19 you walk through a logged area where new plants grow in more sunlight than they could have enjoyed before the trees were cut. Responsible logging such as this also increases forage for wildlife.

You are almost to the end of your walk, and will soon realize that you are once again on Old Daniels Hill Road. At the framed map and the trailbook box, turn left to walk downhill to your car.

If you'd like to know more about the Colony family, their homes are now museums in the city of Keene. You'll find the home of "young" Horatio at 199 Main Street, where you can reflect on the life of a nineteenth-century gentleman of leisure. The Colony House Museum at 104 West Street exhibits collections of glass and pottery produced locally between 1871 and 1923. You'll also see china tableware brought down the Connecticut River from Canada by boat during the early 1890s, silver pieces, and a unique collection of miniature wood turnings. There are Civil War relics and a collection of American Revolution–era documents and manuscripts.

39. Little Monadnock Mountain

Walking distance: 2.2 miles
Walking time: 2 hours
Fitzwilliam, New Hampshire

THIS WONDERFUL LITTLE MOUNTAIN RISES ON THE Metacomet-Monadnock Trail, just before its terminus at Grand Monadnock Mountain. The trail begins at Meriden, Connecticut, and if you want you can walk 160 miles along the Connecticut River, over Mount Tom, the Holyoke range and the Northfield hills in Massachusetts, then up into New Hampshire over Little Monadnock, Gap Mountain, and finally, the Grand Monadnock.

The walk up Little Monadnock takes you through part of Rhododendron State Park and its wild landscape, gradually uphill through pine and hemlock forest, beeches and birches, past old stone walls, and up to some great ledges that look across a valley to Pack Monadnock and Grand Monadnock. It's a worthwhile walk for little effort, although you may question my opinion as you climb a couple of short but steep grades. Notice the giant pines along this walk. They're quite remarkable.

ACCESS

From Keene travel south approximately 12 miles on NH 12 to a junction with NH 119 at Fitzwilliam. Turn right on NH 119, travel west to Rhododendron Road, and turn right again. Cross an intersecting road at 1.9 miles (there's a cemetery on the right) and keep going straight ahead for approximately 1.2 miles to a sign for the park, on your right. Turn right and pass the small brown house on your left. Follow the sign to the parking lot and picnic area. Travelers coming from other directions will find it easy to locate NH 119 on a road map. It runs west to east from Brattleboro, Vermont, to West Rindge, New Hampshire, about 5 miles north of the Massachusetts border.

155

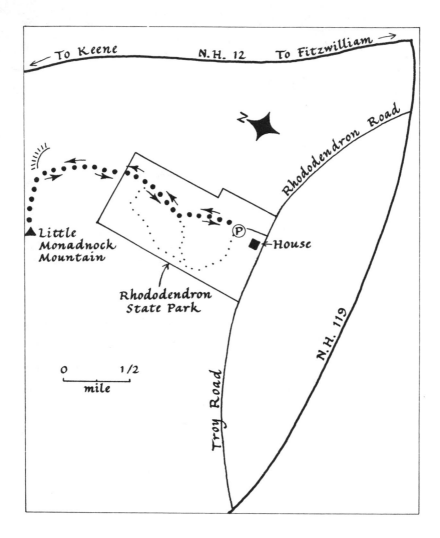

TRAIL

The trail begins on the right side of the parking lot. Face the Rhododendron Park Loop Trail sign and then follow the path it indicates for about ten minutes to signs for Little Monadnock and the Metacomet-Monadnock Trail. The trail is well blazed from here on (and throughout the New Hampshire section of the Metacomet-Monadnock Trail) with white paint oblongs on trees. It's easy to follow

156

as it winds through dense woods of hemlock, oak, and beeches, and past those giant pines.

As you go uphill you'll catch a view from a large boulder down onto a valley floor. Stop here and catch your breath. The stone wall you'll soon follow once ran along a farmer's pasture. Go up another small hill and under a downed tree to a sign stating that you are now leaving the State Park.

The trail continues through the wall and over rocks. Wild oats, blueberries, and Indian cucumber root bloom here in the spring. Juniper bushes give further evidence that this was once farmland. Scramble up some steep rocks and down to a brook that will be dry in midsummer unless there's been a lot of rain. Bear left over the brook. The bells of Solomon's seal weigh their graceful stems nearly horizontal on a steep rise. The path bears left. You'll see mountain laurel on the side of the trail, lots of goldthread, and princes pine on the ground.

The stone wall and the trail along it carry you up again, northwest to a boundary stake, where you turn right through a break in the wall. In a few minutes the trail winds back toward the wall, which now stays on your left. The hill levels out as you walk along the ridge, and after an easy walk of about eight more minutes you come out onto the ledges to enjoy the fine view.

Did you ever see a flock of dragon flies? They danced over our heads for half an hour as we sat on these ledges just below the summit.

Return the way you came. When you reach the trail signs at the bottom, turn right to enjoy the rest of the Rhododendron Loop and the Wildflower Trail, which will lead you back to your car. (See the "Rhododendron State Park" walk in this book).

40. Rhododendron State Park

Walking distance: about ¾ mile
Walking time: 1 hour
Fitzwilliam, New Hampshire

A SMALL FOREST HAS BEEN SET ASIDE BY THE state of New Hampshire to conserve the largest display of native *Rhododendron maximum* in the northeastern United States. The state maintains a wide and comfortable path for visitors to walk on, and the Garden Club of Fitzwilliam has built and maintains a wildflower trail which has won national awards. The rhododendron blooms are at their best in mid-July, but you can see a wealth of flower varieties from early spring until the bright berries and foliage of fall. Many birds are at home here, as are rabbits, squirrels, skunk, and deer. Picnic tables, toilets, and ample parking space add to the park's hospitality. Arrangements can be made for wheelchair-bound people to view the park. Call John Twitchell at 603-239-8153.

Belonging to the heath family, rhododendrons are related to blueberries, cranberries, mountain laurel, heathers, trailing arbutus, and wintergreen. New Hampshire is home to five native rhododendrons: the rosebay or *Rhododendron maximum*, rhodora, swamp azalea, June pink azalea, and Lapland rosebay, all of which usually grow only in isolated locations. In this park, the largest of these natives grow to great heights in dense stands. Their long, thick leaves absorb as much light as possible through the summer months. In winter the leaves curl and droop to conserve moisture.

The garden variety rhododendrons we are most familiar with are hybridized from these and others of an estimated 10,000 species of the rhododendron genus growing around the world.

The National Park Service has declared Rhododendron State Park a National Natural Landmark.

ACCESS

From Keene travel south approximately 12 miles on NH 12 to the junction with NH 119 at Fitzwilliam. Turn right on NH 119 and go

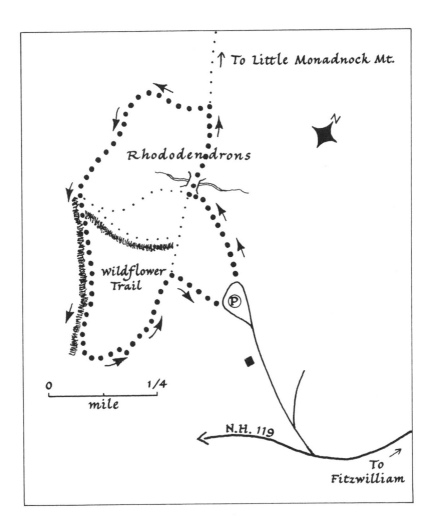

To Little Monadnock Mt.

Rhododendrons

wildflower
Trail

P

0   1/4
     mile

N.H. 119

To
Fitzwilliam

west to Rhododendron Road on your right. Cross a road after 1.9 miles (there's a cemetery on the right-hand side) and soon reach a sign for the park on your right. Turn into the park. Pass a small brown house on your left, and follow a sign to the parking lot and picnic area.

Travelers coming from other directions will find it easy to locate NH 119 on a road map. The road runs from west to east from Brattleboro, Vermont to West Rindge, New Hampshire, about 5 miles north of the Massachusetts border.

TRAIL

The trails around the park are clearly marked and well maintained. There are benches you can sit on to rest and enjoy the splendid plants all around you. Begin your walk on the trail at the right-hand corner of the parking lot. Walk first through a forest of spruce, towering pine, and hemlock. On the ground are dewberry, pyrola, Canada mayflower, bunchberry, and partridgeberry. The rhododendron bushes will amaze you by their size. In about ten minutes you come to a sign for Little Monadnock Mountain. Turn left here. You're surrounded by dense rhododendron growth for as far as you can see. The open blossoms are dainty. The closed blossoms look like tiny pineapples tinged with dark pink.

Cross a wooden bridge over a slow brook, then go up a small rise and bear left past a bench. A Loop Trail sign appears on the left, and the Wildflower Trail sign directs you ahead to identify and enjoy the flowers specially marked for you. The Garden Club of Fitzwilliam continues to develop this trail, and you'll see some marked plants that have been planted by club members, though most grow here naturally.

When you reach a fork in the path, turn right to return to your car. Refreshed by all this beauty, relax and enjoy a picnic lunch at one of the shaded tables before you leave.

Since the rhododendrons remain green all year, this would make an attractive ski tour.

41. Chesterfield Gorge

Walking distance: ¾ mile
Walking time: 1 hour or less
Chesterfield, New Hampshire

ALONGSIDE US 9, BETWEEN KEENE, NEW HAMP-
shire, and Brattleboro, Vermont, there's what appears to be nothing
more than a wayside stop with picnic tables. This is the starting point
for a jewel of a walk beside a spectacular gorge and a string of tumbling
waterfalls. Wildflowers bloom here in season, and there are several
varieties of trees. The whole scene presents excellent opportunities
for photographers at every time of year.

ACCESS

Take US 9 either east or west until you're about 6 miles west of Keene,
or 8 miles east of the Brattleboro exit on I-91. You'll see a sign on
the north side of the road that says Chesterfield Gorge Wayside Area
and space for parking.

TRAIL

Follow the path that leads to the right past the picnic tables, and
proceed through oak, birch, and white pine forest—be careful not to
break the aerial tramway a spider spun across your trail in the early
morning. A sign soon tells you to turn left, past a beech and a maple
tree, onto the Gorge Trail and into a hemlock woods. The next sign
you'll reach has two arrows on it. Keep on the path that leads to the
right, and then go left along the length of the brook, where you'll
catch numerous fine views down into the gorge. After about ten minutes of walking you can take a picture of the highest waterfall in the
gorge.

There have been erosion problems here and the wet rocks are slippery, so fences have been erected along the walk to protect both you
and the gorge. Walk about twenty minutes more, down a long hill to
the brook and across the wooden bridge to the other side. Head uphill

161

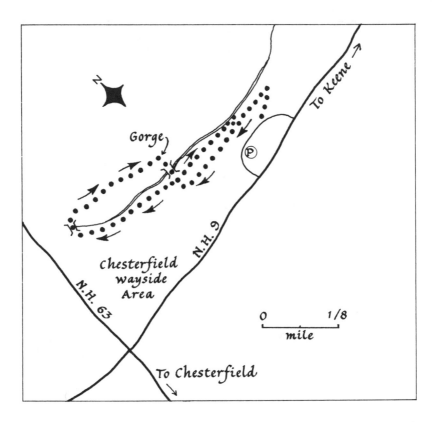

to your right, along more fence. Looking back across the brook, you can see a rockslide that clearly demonstrates the need to protect this unique place. The views from this side are more spectacular than those from the other side. Lacy ferns and vines hang from the cliffs. Two caves in the cliff may intrigue you. One waterfall after the next leads you onward until, too quickly, you cross another bridge back to the other side of the brook.

Follow an unmarked path to your left, moving gently uphill high above the brook. You'll see clearings below that look like perfect places for relaxing beside the water. A path leads you along the bank and then down to these clearings. When you're ready to leave, come back up to where you started down and turn right to meet the path on which you began this walk. Turn left, then sharp right at the trail sign and the maple and beech trees. Walk uphill to the parking area and your car.

162

A spectacular gorge and then a string of tumbling waterfalls.

42. The Kilburn Loop in Pisgah State Park

Walking distance: 6 miles
Walking time: 4 hours
Chesterfield, New Hampshire

SOUTHWEST OF KEENE, NEW HAMPSHIRE, AND northeast of Brattleboro, Vermont, between Chesterfield and Hinsdale, New Hampshire, 13,000 acres of beautiful forest spread over low ridges and around picturesque ponds and streams. Chief Justice Harlan Fisk Stone was born in a house whose foundation lies near the northern entrance to the park. There are four designated parking places from which to enter the park, depending on which trail and which activity you're after. You can walk, ski, snowshoe, or snowmobile, as well as use other motorized off-road vehicles within park boundaries. However, not all activities are allowed on all trails.

The Kilburn Loop Trail is also a ski trail. It's marked for you by blue patches on trees.

ACCESS

From Keene follow NH 9 west and pass Spofford to reach a junction with NH 63. Turn left. Travel south through the village of Chesterfield. Two and one-half miles south of there is a dirt road on the left, with space to park. Signs and a barricade in front of you indicate the quite informal entrance to the park and Kilburn Road.

You can also travel north on NH 63, 2.5 miles past Hinsdale. Of course, the entrance to your trailhead will then be on the right-hand side of the road.

TRAIL

The dirt road straight ahead of you as you pass the barricade is Kilburn Road, which will connect with the Kilburn Loop Trail in a few minutes. Birds sing to you as you amble up the old road for about .6 mile

164

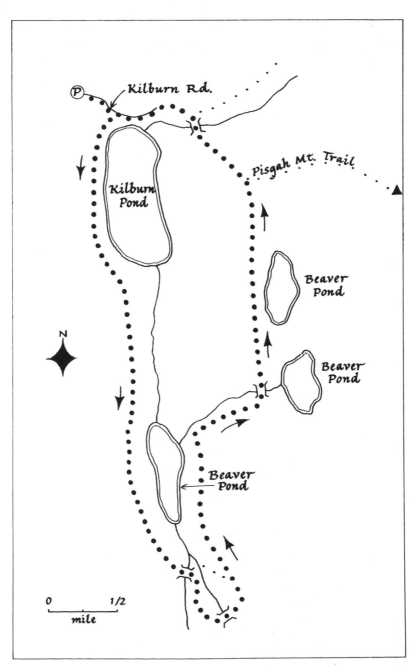

through beeches, birches, and maples. Along the edge of the road ferns mix with glossy-leaved mountain laurel bearing its tiny, pink, umbrella flowers. Graceful hemlock trees surround you. You'll see many granite ledges on this walk. Climb a long, gradual hill with a deep ravine on your right. Blue paint on trees on both sides of you mark the park border, and a sign above reads, "Entering Pisgah State Park." The road curves to the right, and five minutes later you'll see the Kilburn Loop sign.

Turn right onto the loop trail. You'll see suggestions of paths trampled on your left down to the pond inlet, where the tight buds of the yellow bullhead lily float on the water in mid-June. Hobblebush shares the roadside with mountain laurel. As you walk along the pond, which is a public water supply, you'll see other paths leading to it through open woods. Leatherleaf bushes line its shores, and pink rhodora and blueberry blossoms help to decorate the rocks on the water's edge.

The giant granite boulders across the lake were rounded by glaciers centuries ago.

At the end of the pond there's a clearing where the pointed stubs of trees and some downed trunks with pointed ends tell you that beavers have been hard at work here. A little exploration might lead you to their dam or lodge.

The trail bends to the right away from the water now, then immediately left. Watch for the blue blaze. There's a brook that leaves the pond and runs below you, parallel to the trail, its small cascades splashing in the sunlight. Follow the trail down a hill, then up again high above the brook. There's more mountain laurel to delight you, and more hemlock woods. You'll see a rather swampy pond through the woods below you. The path narrows. The brook is with you again, and you walk down a long incline to it and turn right to cross it via an old wooden bridge. You'll see a new log bridge, too. You're about one hour from where you began your walk.

The trail bears right uphill, and then winds around and down to the left to cross a second old bridge with side rails along it. Now a left fork returns to the brook, but you bear right up a gradual hill, which levels out for a minute high above the brook again. There are blueberries on the trailside here, and a blanket of club moss. Notice the very big boulders in the woods. Go uphill again away from the brook, but you can see another swampy area through the trees. Stop to hear the bullfrogs give a concert, or the wood thrushes trill their melodies.

166

Tight buds of yellow bullhead lilies float on the water in the middle of June.

The hemlocks throughout this forest are lovely. Some of them are very tall and straight. The younger ones are short, and their branches dance in breezes beside your path. You'll arrive at the brook again. There's a beaver pond, or the remains of one, ahead of you. Bright green ferns grow across a dam that beavers built. On your left another wooden bridge leads you across the brook once more. There's a freshly beaver-chewed tree on the left, and on your right a big old chewed tree on the ground.

The trail runs gradually uphill all the way now, through some knee-high ferns and a beech forest, and then hemlocks again. A great flat rock on a curve in the path will make a good resting place. Then the trail curves to the right and to the left, and to the right again (you need to watch carefully for the blue patches here). Go left at the bottom of a downhill and away to the left from another swamp. Walk parallel to the swamp you see through the trees, and reach a junction and signs for the Pisgah Mountain Trail. Keep straight across the trail toward Kilburn Road, following yellow patches now instead of blue ones.

In about fifteen minutes the trail narrows. Shoulder-high hemlocks border your path. You'll reach another junction where a sign indicates that you are .3 mile from Kilburn Loop trailhead, and .8 mile from the Kilburn Road trailhead where you began your walk. The road is grassy; you're out of the dense woods and into sunlight. You reach the sign where you entered the loop and the road you came in on. Another .6 mile of the laurel-edged road will complete this good, long walk.

For another hike in this park, see the description in Daniel Doan's *50 More Hikes in New Hampshire* (Backcountry Publications); to enjoy the Kilburn Loop as a ski tour, see *25 Ski Tours in New Hampshire* (Backcountry Publications) by Roioli Schweiker.

43. Wantastiquet Mountain

Walking distance: 4 miles
Walking time: 2½ hours
Hinsdale, New Hampshire

THIS EASILY ACCESSIBLE MOUNTAIN ON THE NEW
Hampshire side of the Connecticut River and its tributary, the Wells
River, towers above the city of Brattleboro, Vermont. The gradually
ascending trail to its summit will take you on a pleasant walk through
hemlock and hardwood forests, spring wildflowers, and interesting
geological formations.

ACCESS

Travel west on NH 19, 6.5 miles from its junction with NH 63 in
Hinsdale, New Hampshire. Just before a bridge over the Connecticut
River, there's a right-hand turn onto a dirt road marked simply "Dead
End." Drive .2 mile to a parking space on your right. Your trail
begins here.

If you travel from Brattleboro, drive toward the river. Cross railroad
tracks and two green bridges and turn left on the dirt road. Travel
the .2 mile to the parking place mentioned above.

TRAIL

Walk north through the green gate and past a high, tumbling waterfall.

Continue up a long, gradual climb. There are several views of the
river along the way. Be sure to ignore side paths and stay on the road,
which switches several times to the north and south before it reaches
the summit. The woods here are beeches, hemlocks, and oaks. In
about ten minutes you come to a great ledge you can climb for your
first river view. Then walk north again, bearing right at an old sign.
The path is bordered now by lush hemlocks on either side. Slate
ledges protrude from the banks. Bright green mountain laurel grows
profusely along your trail. In another five minutes you're high above

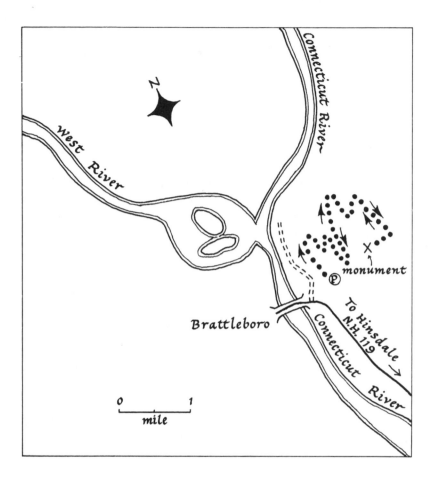

the river and the city. The town clock rings the hour. A line of trucks hums far below you on the highway.

Red blazes on trees indicate a border of some kind—stay on the road. In another five minutes the hemlocks give way to a predominantly hardwood forest with an abundance of oaks. You can see farms along the river. In the fall, yellow witch hazel blossoms bend over the path. Ground pines grow at your feet. The road curves to the right past a bank of laurel growing high up the hill to massive granite ledges. You come to another switchback, and now denser laurel bushes hug both sides of the road. You meet the red border blazes again. The laurel grows so beautifully among the rocks that it looks as though it

170

The town clock tolls the hour.

had been skillfully planted. The scenery gets rockier. Notice the great boulders decked in rock tripe, which the deer browse on.

You can feel that you're near the summit. The trail leads southward and up the last long hill to a level ridge. Just before the road starts downhill again, there's a path to the right that climbs up some ledges to an open summit. Beside you is a monument, "to Walter H. Child from his friends, erected in 1908." Below you the river is a wide gray ribbon, and Brattleboro is a toy town. Tiny cars speed along I-91. On the way down, if it's spring, enjoy the mayflowers; if it's fall, kick the leaves; and in winter, appreciate the leafless trees that allow you views of the river all the way back.

44. The Sunrise Trail—Fort Dummer State Park

Walking distance: 1.2 miles
Walking time: 45 minutes
Brattleboro, Vermont

IN 1724 THIS SECTION OF VERMONT STILL BE-
longed to Massachusetts. Indians were a threat to the white settlers, so the Massachusetts General Court voted to build a fort to protect its settlements in the vicinity of Northfield, Massachusetts and Hinsdale, New Hampshire. William Dummer, the acting governor of the Massachusetts Bay Colony, ordered the fort to be built; hence its name. It was once the most important trading post in northern Massachusetts, and the town of Dummer Meadows was the first permanent English settlement in Vermont. The meadows and the site of the fort now lie beneath the backed-up waters of the Vernon dam. The monument that commemorates the Fort, down on the Connecticut River shore at the southern end of Brattleboro, and Fort Dummer State Park, above the river, remain as memorials to an important defensive outpost of the early colonies.

The walk on the Sunrise Trail is short but rewarding, with abundant birds and flowers, and a wide variety of trees. There are also a couple of wide panoramas of the Connecticut River.

Meeting interesting people is one of the pleasures of hiking. A young German couple that we met on our walk told of their many surprises on their first trip to America. The country is so big; they wished they had known of New England's beauty earlier in their trip; they were shocked at the amount of litter and the lack of public transportation. They were traveling by Greyhound's America program, which is fine for cities, but difficult if you want to get off the beaten track. Next time they will rent a car.

ACCESS

From the junction of I-91 and US 5 at Brattleboro (Exit 1), go .1 mile

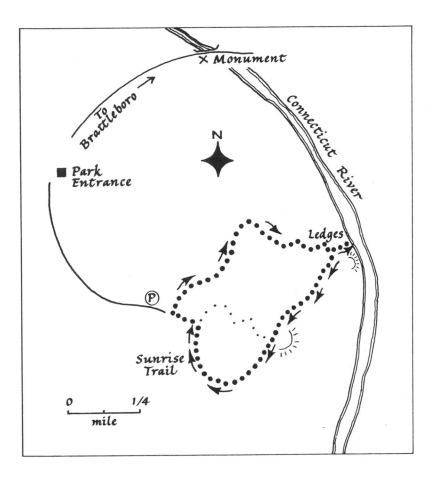

north on US 5 and then .5 mile east on Fairground Road, to a junction with South Main Street. Drive 1.1 mile south on South Main Street, up over a long hill to the well-marked park entrance. There is a small entrance fee, for which you will receive a trail map and parking directions.

TRAIL

The Sunrise Trail commences down an old road whose trees are well blazed with blue patches. An open woods stretches out on both sides of you. Ferns catch the sunlight. Dark shiny wintergreen leaves accent

173

A sunlit road through open woods.

the paler leaves of blueberries beneath oaks and birches. The trail winds through the forest and down to a brook, where it crosses a small wooden bridge.

Follow the blue blazes around to the left and soon you'll reach a side trail marked by yellow blazes. Follow this trail uphill across a small ridge to some granite ledges and a wide-open space where you can see across the Connecticut River to New Hampshire. This is an ideal spot to sit in the sun, eat lunch, or meditate.

Return to the blue-blazed trail. Go left uphill, past a bank of ground pines, to another ridge. You may see trees in the woods wrapped in burlap, with metal tags above the burlap. A yellow plastic bug catcher hangs on a branch. The Vermont Forest Service conducts experiments here in the interest of controlling Japanese beetles, tent caterpillars, and pear thrips.

174

Continue your walk on the main trail. A marked trail on your right would take you back down on a slightly shorter walk than if you kept straight ahead. Almost opposite this side trail you'll come to another open view of the river and hills in Massachusetts. If you choose the longer way down, keep straight ahead, around a great loop, through more hemlock forest. You'll see several varieties of mushrooms if it's been damp.

Though this walk is nice in the summer, you should also take it when the leaves are nearly pastel colored in the spring, or mostly yellow, lighting up the autumn woods, or when the dark green of the hemlocks accents the whiteness of the snow.

The blue blazes lead you easily, but too soon, back to where you began.

Guidebooks from The Countryman Press and Backcountry Publications

Written for people of all ages and experience, these popular and carefully prepared books feature detailed trail and tour directions, notes on points of interest and natural phenomena, maps and photographs.

WALKS AND RAMBLES SERIES

Walks and Rambles on the Delmarva Peninsula, $8.95
Walks and Rambles in Rhode Island, $8.95
Walks and Rambles in Westchester (NY) and Fairfield (CT) Counties, $7.95

BIKING SERIES

25 Mountain Bike Tours in Vermont, $9.95
25 Bicycle Tours on Delmarva, $8.95
25 Bicycle Tours in Eastern Pennsylvania, $8.95
20 Bicycle Tours in the Finger Lakes, $7.95
25 Bicycle Tours in the Hudson Valley, $9.95
25 Bicycle Tours in Maine, $8.95
25 Bicycle Tours in New Hampshire, $7.95
25 Bicycle Tours in New Jersey, $8.95
20 Bicycle Tours in and around New York City, $7.95
25 Bicycle Tours in Vermont, $8.95

CANOEING SERIES

Canoe Camping Vermont and New Hampshire Rivers, $7.95
Canoeing Central New York, $10.95
Canoeing Massachusetts, Rhode Island and Connecticut, $7.95

HIKING SERIES

50 Hikes in the Adirondacks, $10.95
50 Hikes in Central New York, $9.95
50 Hikes in Central Pennsylvania, $9.95
50 Hikes in Connecticut, $9.95
50 Hikes in Eastern Pennsylvania, $10.95
50 Hikes in the Hudson Valley, $9.95
50 Hikes in Massachusetts, $9.95
50 More Hikes in New Hampshire, $9.95
50 Hikes in New Jersey, $10.95
50 Hikes in Northern Maine, $10.95
50 Hikes in Southern Maine, $10.95
50 Hikes in Vermont, 3rd edition, $9.95
50 Hikes in West Virginia, $9.95
50 Hikes in Western Pennsylvania, $9.95
50 Hikes in the White Mountains, $9.95

ADIRONDACK SERIES

Discover the Adirondack High Peaks, $14.95
Discover the Central Adirondacks, $8.95
Discover the Eastern Adirondacks, $9.95
Discover the Northeastern Adirondacks, $9.95
Discover the Northern Adirondacks, $10.95
Discover the Northwestern Adirondacks, $11.95
Discover the South Central Adirondacks, $8.95
Discover the Southeastern Adirondacks, $8.95
Discover the Southern Adirondacks, $9.95
Discover the Southwestern Adirondacks, $9.95
Discover the West Central Adirondacks, $13.95

SKI-TOURING SERIES

25 Ski Tours in Central New York, $7.95
25 Ski Tours in New Hampshire, $8.95

OTHER GUIDES

Maine: An Explorer's Guide, 4th edition, $14.95
New England's Special Places, $10.95
New York State's Special Places, $12.95
The Other Massachusetts: An Explorer's Guide, $12.95
State Parks and Campgrounds in Northern New York, $9.95
Vermont: An Explorer's Guide, 3rd edition, $14.95

The above titles are available at bookstores and at certain sporting goods stores or may be ordered directly from the publisher. For complete descriptions of these and other guides, write: The Countryman Press, P.O. Box 175, Woodstock, VT 05091.